D0205257

EASY SEWING FOR INFANTS
BY LEILA ALBALA

SEVENTH EDITION, COMPLETELY REVISED

ALPEL PUBLISHING, CHAMBLY, QUEBEC, CANADA

EASY SEWING FOR INFANTS
by Leila Albala
Seventh edition, completely revised

Other books by Leila Albala:
Easy Sewing for Children (75 patterns)
Easy Sewing for Adults (78 patterns)
Easy Halloween Costumes for Children (60 costumes)
Costumes d'Halloween Pour Enfants (French edition)
Catalogue of Canadian Catalogues

Although every effort has been made to make this book as accurate as possible, the author and ALPEL PUBLISHING shall have neither liability nor responsibility to any person or entity with respect to any loss or damage caused, or allegedly caused, directly or indirectly by the information contained in this book.

All rights reserved. No part of this book may be reproduced or transmitted in any form or by any means, electronic or mechanical, including photocopying, or by any information storage or retrieval system, without permission in writing from the Publisher, except by a reviewer, who may quote brief passages in a review.

Layout by Elie Albala

Cover design by Albert Albala

Copyright © 1982, 1983, 1988 Leila Albala

Canadian Cataloguing in Publication Data

    Albala, Leila
      Easy sewing for infants

    7th ed.
    Includes index.
    ISBN 0-921993-00-5

    1. Infants--Clothing. 2. Sewing.
    I. Title.

    TT715.A42 1988   646.4'06   C87-090273-3

Printed in Canada

"Fully detailed illustrations and simple instructions. Great selection of patterns. A must for every mother-to-be, mother and grandmother." (Vogue Patterns)

"Easy enlargement, expert sewing tips." (Family Circle)

"My kind of pattern book. Beautifully organized, you can read it like a menu - and count up your savings at the same time." (Kathy Faryon, Times Colonist)

"Straightforward, no-nonsense presentation of material, easy-do layouts of diagrams, clear directions, easy to adapt, change or modify." (Catalog Sources, News & Updates)

"Excellent basic patterns, easy to follow, guarantee they'll save you money, splendid system for enlarging patterns." (Crafts Review, The Best and Newest in Craft Supplies and Products)

"Large selection of patterns, nicely illustrated." (National Home Business Report)

"Without doubt the best self-published books I have ever encountered and just as good as any of the professional sewing books on the market." (Hands Magazine)

"Can't imagine life without Leila's books." (Joyce Schimmel)

"Proved their worth many times over, common-sense approach most refreshing. More, more!!" (D. Forrest Wilton)

"Your book has been more useful than all my other sewing books!" (Lise Aumais)

"I am a total amateur at sewing but can follow your patterns so easily. I am impressed!" (M. Marth)

"Inspired by simplicity and common-sense approach." (D. Attenborough)

"Very easy, just perfect for me." (Nicole Roy)

"Your books are great, especially for children. I don't always want an elaborate pattern. I want to finish it before they grow out of it!" (Ann Doucet)

"Hallelujah at long last!!!" (Cathy Stuart)

"In 16 years of sewing, I have never encountered anything so useful and informative as your book." (Nancy Hendrickson)

ACKNOWLEDGEMENTS

Each member of my family has contributed to make the writing and illustrating of this book a very interesting and rewarding experience. I am dedicating this book to my children, Albert and Rina.

My husband, Elie, has been emotionally supportive, encouraging and helpful in many ways. He is also my business partner who shares the work load of hundreds of practical details in our publishing business. My son Albert (who was seven when I wrote the first edition), often helped by taking care of his little sister in order to give me peace to write. He also boosted my efforts with his sincere compliments expressing how proud he is to have such a smart mommy, able to write a real book! And finally, my daughter Rina (then 18 months old) was such an active and curious little "helper". She climbed cheerfully on the table to steal my pen, tear my precious patterns and close my typewriter, interrupting me a hundred times to play with her. And yet she contributed in her own unique way. She was my main source of inspiration for these patterns. Without her, I wouldn't have even thought of starting to write this first book which has led to the writing of several other pattern books.

Aside from my own children, I would also like to thank Alicia, Paul, Marlyn, Anne, and their mothers, and especially my good friends Juliet Gauthier, Susan Bélanger, and Shelly Fabian for their help. Special thanks to Jeanette Paul for her dedicated copyediting and proofreading.

Finally, thank you, my readers. Your supportive and enthusiastic letters have given me an incredible amount of energy as well as a perfect reason to continue writing these pattern books.

Leila Albala

VISUAL PATTERN INDEX

PATTERN NUMBER UNDER EACH DESIGN.   PAGE NUMBER IN PARENTHESIS.

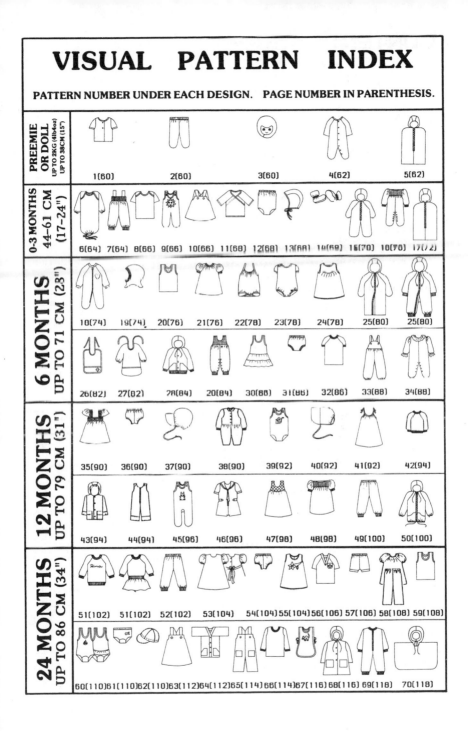

PREEMIE OR DOLL UP TO 2KG (4lb 4oz) UP TO 38CM (15")

1(60) 2(60) 3(60) 4(62) 5(62)

0-3 MONTHS 44-61 CM (17-24")

6(64) 7(64) 8(66) 9(66) 10(66) 11(68) 12(68) 13(68) 14(68) 15(70) 16(70) 17(72)

6 MONTHS UP TO 71 CM (28")

18(74) 19(74) 20(76) 21(76) 22(78) 23(78) 24(78) 25(80) 25(80)

26(82) 27(82) 28(84) 29(84) 30(86) 31(86) 32(86) 33(88) 34(88)

12 MONTHS UP TO 79 CM (31")

35(90) 36(90) 37(90) 38(90) 39(92) 40(92) 41(92) 42(94)

43(94) 44(94) 45(96) 46(96) 47(98) 48(98) 49(100) 50(100)

24 MONTHS UP TO 86 CM (34")

51(102) 51(102) 52(102) 53(104) 54(104) 55(104) 56(106) 57(106) 58(108) 59(108)

60(110) 61(110) 62(110) 63(112) 64(112) 65(114) 66(114) 67(116) 68(116) 69(118) 70(118)

CONTENTS

PATTERNS FOR PREEMIE OR DOLL

PATTERNS FOR 0-3 MONTH-OLDS

PATTERNS FOR 6-MONTH-OLDS

PATTERNS FOR 12-MONTH-OLDS

PATTERNS FOR 24-MONTH-OLDS

TO THE READER

Welcome to the world of miniature patterns. Whether you are an old pro or a beginner, you will discover that it is a smart, "new" way of pattern-making. While I cannot claim to have invented miniature patterns, it is unusual to find a whole book full of them. Although they have been popular in Scandinavia and many European countries for years, I was cautioned that Canadian and American sewers insist on full-size patterns. I decided, however, to take the risk with a pattern book for infants firmly believing there must be a few sewers interested in the miniature method. And there are. Not just a few, but more than 40,000 ordered my book after reading about it in Family Circle, Vogue Patterns, and several other magazines. That first pattern book has grown into a series of books. They are still available by mail order, and now through many public libraries, book stores and fabric outlets, too.

I am particularly pleased by the testimonials from some of my readers who had no previous experience with miniature patterns (or sewing either!), and yet had enough courage and curiosity to try them. They were rewarded by the discovery that this is an easy and creative method. Each miniature pattern takes only minutes to enlarge.

A huge, ever-growing pile of letters from my readers never fails to give me energy and encouragement. This positive demand for miniature patterns reflects my own desire to have such books myself. It is practical to have a large selection of basic, versatile patterns on hand. This book saves time and money, not only in isolated areas, but for busy and creative hands everywhere.

I wish each one of you, my sewing friends, happy and ever easier sewing!

BEFORE YOU START

Before using the patterns in this book, read the text pages with a highlighter pen in hand. Mark all the information that's new and important to you.

For your convenience, I have arranged each pattern and its sewing instructions on adjoining pages. As a bonus, I filled any leftover space with useful sewing tips.

Use the handy index at the end of this book to find any specific information you need.

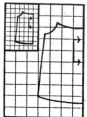

ENLARGING MINIATURE PATTERNS

To include a large selection of designs in my books, each pattern is reduced in size and printed on a miniature grid.

"Easy Sewing for Infants": One square = 2.5cm (1")
"Easy Sewing for Children": One square = 2.5cm (1")
"Easy Sewing for Adults": One square = 5cm (2")

Enlarge miniature patterns to full-size grid by marking all corners, and then connecting them dot-to-dot with lines as shown in the miniature pattern. Once you get used to it, each pattern takes just minutes to enlarge.

The easiest way to enlarge miniature patterns is by taping a sheet of tracing paper on a cardboard cutting board that is marked with a grid. Since the lines on a cardboard cutting board are marked 2½cm (1") apart, reinforce every second line with a black marker so you will also have a 5cm (2") grid for adult patterns.

Or make yourself a handy "master grid" from a large sheet of paper or white vinyl. Draw a grid of squares (2½cm/1") by using a long ruler and a black marker. (Use waterproof marker for vinyl.) If you draw every second line dotted (or use different color), you also have a 5cm (2") grid for adult patterns. Tape a sheet of tracing paper onto your "master grid" (the grid is visible through the paper) and enlarge the miniature patterns (as well as make any alterations) directly onto the tracing paper. The grid remains clean and reusable for years to come. Roll it up for easy storage into any cardboard tube. As a bonus, your "master grid" can be used to enlarge miniature patterns for toys and crafts published in many magazines. Ready-made vinyl grids are also available commercially.

Some fabric stores sell pattern paper or non-woven material (looks like interfacing) marked with dots that are spaced 2.5cm (1") apart. Such paper or material can be used to enlarge miniature patterns by connecting the dots for a grid.

When enlarging many patterns, it is practical to have a good supply of tracing paper on hand. Your local art supply retailer sells tracing paper in large rolls.

Alternatives to tracing paper:

Crinkle-type plastic bags (semi-transparent) that the stores use for your fabrics and other purchases make handy "tracing paper" at literally no cost. Open the bags out flat and tape them together side-by-side. Get your family and friends to collect a supply of such bags for you.

Tissue paper (sheets used for gift wrapping) or wax paper can be used as tracing paper. Tape sheets together.

Old commercial patterns. Here's a source of perfect tracing paper that just might be sitting idle in your house, if you are absolutely sure never to need those patterns again. You might also find commercial patterns for pennies at garage and rummage sales, thrift shops, and your local sewing supply store. The tissue paper sheets are conveniently large so, by ignoring all lines and markings on them and by using bright felt markers, you can use the sheets for your own patterns.

Sometimes you can save pattern paper by enlarging only a part of a pattern. For this reason, I have drawn only half of the patterns (even sleeves) that have identical other halves. When back and front are identical except for neckline (and sometimes front edges too), I have drawn them as one so you need to enlarge only one pattern piece instead of two. (See "Cutting the fabric" for more information.) When the pattern is long and straight or even slightly flared from underarms to hem (such as a dress, long nightgown, T-shirt, bathrobe), enlarge the pattern for the upper part only, and extend cutting lines for the rest directly onto the fabric.

When the pattern is very easy, square or rectangle, such as a gathered skirt, ruffle, waistband or pocket, enlarge it directly onto the fabric to save time and pattern paper. If you are inexperienced in this and afraid that you wouldn't have enough fabric if you cut it without a proper plan, first make a miniature cutting layout with proportional dimensions on any squared paper.

SAVE THE PATTERNS

You will hopefully be able to use many of these patterns several times because, with different fabrics, trims, and variations mentioned in patterns, you can create several different garments from every pattern. The pattern sizes are easy to enlarge and reduce when necessary. Fold the enlarged patterns neatly into separate envelopes (used envelopes are fine), and mention the pattern name, number, size, and the page number of this book for easy reference on each envelope. Mention pattern numbers also on each pattern piece in case they get mixed up. Straighten out folded pattern pieces with warm iron.

FABRIC REQUIREMENTS
SUGGESTED FABRICS

There are no cutting layouts in this book because they would take up so much space that I would have to eliminate many patterns. I have mentioned the fabric requirements for the most likely, or most convenient fabric width for each pattern, always mentioning first the length and then the width. If you use fabric of different width, calculate from the miniature or the enlarged pattern, how much fabric is needed, or take this book or the enlarged pattern with you to the store. Better yet, adopt my style of sewing and stock up on fabrics at home in larger quantities, and then let the fabrics inspire you to see what can be made out of them. Then cut out several garments one day, and sew them the next.

Suggested fabrics are listed for every garment, but be inventive and adventurous and use fabrics of your choice. If you wish to use non-stretch fabric for a pattern designed for stretch fabrics only, enlarge the pattern slightly to add sufficient ease. When using stretch fabrics for a pattern designed for non-stretch fabrics, eliminate seam allowances or reduce the pattern slightly in width if you find it necessary (depending on design).

Extra fabric may be required for stripes, plaids, or one-way designs or for fabric with one-way nap. Fabric requirements are listed only for original design, not for variations mentioned in the brackets. Notions needed to complete each garment (except the thread) are listed.

SIMPLE INSTRUCTIONS

Instructions for completing each garment are purposely kept short and simple to encourage you to realize how easy, uncomplicated, and pleasant sewing can be. Naturally you need to know basic sewing techniques before using patterns with such brief instructions. Let the work guide you rather than intimidate you, and use common sense to solve the little problems that may surface. Practice, of course, is your very best teacher and, although I have been sewing all my life, I am humbly learning all the time.

If you are an inexperienced seamstress, ask a sewing friend for help to give you the confidence so necessary in the beginning. Buy yourself at least one really good sewing instruction book with a comprehensive index, so you'll have your own private teacher at all times. I have several good books with detailed, professional illustrations and up-to-date, easy to understand know-how about practically everything concerning sewing. They are my endless source of useful information.

In order to include so many patterns in this book, I have saved space by using brief, non-repetitive directions. After getting used to this style of sewing, I am confident you will be able to sew without any directions.

It is important to read the text part of this book because I keep referring to it frequently.

Rib knits: See "Rib knit bands".

Patch pockets: Overlock upper edge, fold it under 2.5cm (1") with right sides together, stitch folded ends closed, turn right side out, press, and topstitch upper edge down. Press seam allowances under on both sides and lower edge. Topstitch pockets in place. When sewing a pocket with curved corners, stitch upper edge as explained above, then baste around curves and pull the thread so that the curves turn neatly under; press seam allowances under and topstitch the pocket in place.

Ruffles: When sewing a ruffle to skirt lower edge, stitch ruffle pieces together into a circle. Narrowly hem the lower edge of ruffle, or trim it with lace. Sew two rows of long gathering stitches, close to each other, to ruffle upper edge. Divide both ruffle upper edge and skirt lower edge into equal parts (four to eight sections, depending on skirt width) and mark the sections with pins. With right sides together, match markings, and pin ruffle to garment. Pull bobbin threads of gathering stitches to gather ruffle edge, so that it will match the garment's edge, distributing the fullness evenly. Stitch ruffle to the garment, with gathers up against the presser foot. Zigzag or overlock raw edges of seam allowances together.

Overlock: To cleanfinish raw edges of pocket tops, lower edge of garment, sleeve ends, and facings, overlock (or zigzag) the edge prior to topstitching it in place. This fast and neat method also helps you to avoid excessive bulk since you don't need to fold the raw edges under.

METRIC AND IMPERIAL MEASUREMENTS

This book provides you with both metric and imperial measurements. I always mention first the metric, then the equivalent imperial measurement.

The measurements may differ slightly and, for practical purposes, show rounded figures, but the difference is irrelevant. Confidently choose either system and ignore the other one.

For your convenience. I have listed below fractions of an inch frequently used in sewing and their metric equivalents.

Metric	Imperial
3 mm	1/8"
5 mm	3/16"
6 mm	1/4"
1 cm	3/8"
1.3 cm	1/2"
1.5 cm	5/8"
2 cm	3/4"
2.5 cm	1"

SEWING MACHINES

When I once stayed in Switzerland for two years, I was like an orphan without my sewing machine. Fortunately I found a very old sewing machine at a flea market (for five dollars!). It was one of those non-electric, unbreakable, basic models with a large, decorative table and straight stitch only. I managed to get the tension so good that I was able to sew my wedding gown, winter coat, and many other lovely garments.

With a few other machines since then, I have learned a lot along the way. Choosing the best machine for your purposes is both time consuming and very difficult when the choice is so large. When the time came to buy "the best sewing machine in the world", I decided to take the task seriously in order not to regret my decision. I read the whole Consumer Guide book on sewing machines, tested a dozen different machines, attended demonstrations, had home trials, and questioned everybody I knew who sews. It took several months of active, dedicated searching to find a machine that has been sewing with me without a complaint for well over ten years. Of course there are many other good machines on the market apart from my choice, so it is indeed well worth your time to decide carefully which one of them will be your sewing partner perhaps for the rest of your life.

To compare different models, test as many machines as possible. Be firm and don't let an aggressive salesperson talk you into buying a machine before you have seen several, and have had time to think over your decision. Just the fact that a sewing machine is sold at a discount for a limited time shouldn't push you into buying it unless you would choose that one anyway.

If possible, have a demonstration at home so you can take extra time trying it out in peace. Sometimes you may be allowed to keep the machine at home for a trial period free of obligation. If you do this, be sure you will not be intimidated into buying that machine if you are not absolutely sure you want it. Another good reason to test the machine at home is to check how noisy it is in the home environment. There are often so many people and so much noise in stores that it is impossible to properly hear how much noise the machine makes.

Even more important than noise is, of course, the stitch. To check the tension properly, you should have your own fabric samples including heavy-weight fabrics, lightweight knits, and difficult-to-sew sheers. Stores will give you samples but, because they are usually firm cotton, they will show a good stitch with any machine. To be sure the tension is correct, the stitch should lock between the two layers of fabric, and the link should not be visible on either side. A balanced tension shows even stitches on both sides of fabric. For testing, use fabric samples of solid colors and threads in contrasting colors to make the stitch and any faults more visible. Experiment and adjust the upper thread tension without fear, as well as the bobbin thread tension, until you get desired results. Surprisingly enough, many sewing machine salespeople don't know enough about thread tension, sewing stretchy fabrics, or uses of different needles. To adjust the bobbin thread tension, gradually turn the thread tension knob in the bobbin case until you get a good tension. Take along a sewing friend who knows how to test a machine if you are inexperienced yourself.

Freearm is so useful and necessary that I wouldn't recommend buying a machine without it. Even if you have to pay extra, you won't regret it.

A second-hand machine is a good way to start but only if you manage to get good tension with it. Buying a bad sewing machine could be quite discouraging and could make one "allergic to sewing".

In recent years, many inexpensive and yet surprisingly good machines with convenient utility stitches (including various overlock and stretch stitches) have come onto the market. It is not that important to have several decorative, fancy stitches in a sewing machine (because how many times, really, would you want to sew little dogs or whatever running in a row?). If you are shopping for an inexpensive sewing machine, choose one with good straight stitch, with forward and backward movements, zigzag, stretch stitch, built-in buttonholer, blind stitch, and freearm. They are the most essential features, all else is extra. Also try to get at least one "quick seam" or overlock. It's a stitch that sews the seam and finishes the raw edges simultaneously so you don't have to go down the seam twice. You will be using it a lot. (See the chapter "Stretchy Sewing" for improvised quick seam.)

I often think that if husbands realized how much home-sewing saves, they would run to buy the best machine. Some smart men even sew themselves. Impress your husband by showing him the beautiful garments you can create and sew something for him too. He will have every reason to encourage you and to regard you as a talented lady with golden hands.

Are you already wild about sergers? After I found out about sergers (also called overlock machines),

I went to see one. When I had searched several months for just the right sewing machine, I bought my serger after just five minutes of demonstration. I was so impressed and I still am. The machine itself is small and doesn't look at all impressive. In fact, you wouldn't even believe it is a sewing machine. However, it is a small miracle, saves lots of time, and makes sewing fun. There are several different sergers now on the market and, even if you don't intend to buy one, it is most interesting just to see how they work. Yet a word of caution is necessary here. Don't rush to buy one as your only sewing machine because it just sews seams. Therefore, first you need to buy a regular sewing machine.

My serger has two needles, a knife, and four huge spools of thread. The thread can be a problem because it is expensive to buy large cones of thread in several colors and four of each. But, if you have basic colors, they will blend into almost any fabric and will last for a long time. In a pinch, use blending colored threads just for the chainstitch and whatever you have on hand for the overlock. Factories and factory outlets sometimes sell half-empty cones for pennies. Sergers have no bobbin which, you can imagine, is just wonderful for uninterrupted sewing. One needle sews straight chainstitch, while the other one overlocks the edges that are trimmed simultaneously by the knife. The result is a very neat and professional narrow seam. The machine is so amazingly fast that it is now possible to whip up several garments in a few hours.

When buying a sewing machine or serger, inquire about availability of parts and service, guarantee, and free instructions. Take a course in its use, if available, even if you think you know enough about sewing. I was surprised at how much I learned.

Care for your machine and it will reward you with enjoyable and troublefree sewing. Lubricate it regularly and be sure to use only good quality machine oil. I mention this because I heard about one lady who used cooking oil (would you believe!) for her brand new machine. The result was such a mess that even the guarantee did not pay for the repair. When my machine is tired, noisy, and slow, I give it a good cleaning and oiling, change the needle, and it works like a charm again.

Protect your machine from dust by covering it when not in use. If you don't have a special turndown table, or don't always put the machine away in its carrying case, make a pretty little quilt or coverlet and remember to use it. When you leave the machine, turn it off (or unplug it), especially if you have children in the house.

Clogging and jamming are caused by fabric or thread ends being drawn down into the bobbin compartment. It is most annoying. You can virtually eliminate it by practicing these tips. Change the machine needle frequently. When placing the fabric under the presser foot, turn the handwheel so that the take-up lever is in its highest position and the needle is on its way down with the first stitch. Hold the thread ends firmly and taut to the back. Turn the wheel by hand until the needle goes into the fabric. When sewing sheer or difficult fabrics or lightweight knits, backstitching at the beginning and end of the seam may pull the fabric into the needleplate hole. So, slip a piece of typing paper between the fabric and needleplate to get a good start; rip the paper off after sewing.

If jamming occurs in spite of these tricks, take your time to carefully remove the fabric so it won't tear. If gentle pulling doesn't release the fabric from the needleplate hole, unscrew the needle or remove the bobbin case (if not blocked by the needle) or try removing the needleplate.

Be sure to frequently brush away the packed lint that constantly accumulates around the bobbin compartment and under the needleplate. It can clog the machine and cause stitching problems such as jamming, thread breakage, poorly formed stitches, and it can interfere with dropfeed control. If the needle keeps running despite the fact that you have loosened the handwheel for winding the thread on bobbin, undo the handwheel screw, remove outer part and drop a bit of oil into the handwheel bearing. When you stop sewing even for a few seconds, and even in the middle of a seam, learn to take your foot completely off the pedal. Even the lightest touch on the pedal will tease the motor, eventually causing damage which is expensive to repair.

Read your sewing machine manual carefully and refer to it frequently. Particularly useful is the section which explains possible reasons for common sewing machine problems. A few good tricks can save you many expensive and inconvenient trips to a repair shop.

You will be using the sewing machine more often if it is easily available. If possible, have a place where you can leave the machine as is, in case you have to interrupt your work. When my second child was born, she took over my sewing room. Consequently, I found it too inconvenient to store the machine in a closet or to set it on the kitchen table, only to clear it away again for mealtimes. I found myself using it less and less, until I found a solution. While awaiting the sewing room of my dreams in the basement, I sewed in the bedroom. There I had a handy desk, a comfortable chair, and good lighting to encourage me to use the machine again practically daily.

FABRICS

We are lucky with such a beautiful and abundant, often even bewildering choice of fabrics on the market. It's nice to go shopping for just the right fabric in a well-equipped store, but to save time and money I usually stock up fabrics at home, not only for children's clothes, but for the whole family. I enjoy shopping at factory outlets and discount halls and, when I find fabrics I like at a bargain price, I buy lots of them in different colors (a few metres or yards each), even if I don't know right at that moment what I will make out of them. By using fabrics in two or three solid colors or prints that go well together, I make several different garments out of each and then can mix and match them endlessly.

If there is a garment factory near you, check if they sell any leftover fabrics, threads and other notions, and you might well have found your own treasure chest to return to again and again. Bankruptcy sales (or closing of business) should be your favorites too, if you like bargains. If you live in an isolated area, you probably will find it well worth the trip to drive even a longer distance for a carload of rock-bottom priced fabrics. Take your sewing friends along to share the fun and expenses.

Even my husband has recently become quite an expert on fabrics and often surprises me with beautiful fabrics he finds at sales and factories. Aside from praising him for what a wonderful guy he is, I always let him know which fabrics I like the best to ensure that the future surprises are even more successful.

I also check remnant counters for discontinued fabrics, ends of rolls, and pieces with a small flaw. Remnants are often just the right size for kids' clothes and, by combining two or more colors, I can create unique garments for pennies. I always keep a measuring tape in my shopping bag, as well as current measurements of my children. Clever cutting saves a lot of fabric, so it is best to learn to figure out how much is needed. It is easy with a little practice.

It takes imagination to discover the real treasures among the rest of the cheap fabrics which may often look like a pile of junk, but it can be interesting and certainly well worth all the trouble. Sometimes bargain fabrics need to be washed and ironed before you can fully appreciate them and recognize their true potential. In fact, prior to cutting it is wise to wash (or thoroughly soak] all fabrics to preshrink them, unless you are absolutely sure they will not shrink.

Prewashing serves other purposes too. Some fabrics are pressed off-grain and might be sold at a low price just for that reason. To straighten them, you may need to dampen such fabrics. Stretch gently on the bias and press, if necessary. Often washing sets the fibers straight without trouble. That's why a garment sewn from off-grain fabric appears twisted after washing. If you can't wash or iron out the pressed foldline, avoid that when cutting out the fabric. Or place crease where it is not too visible, or underneath ribbon trim [down center of sweatshirt sleeves or sides of pull-on pants]. Fabrics printed off-grain are impossible to straighten. Prewashing also removes finishes that may cause skipped stitches.

It may seem such a pity to wash or even just soak new fabrics especially since they are probably clean. However, I have never regretted doing so, whereas I have made my share of mistakes by sewing garments without preshrinking the fabric, only to have an unpleasant surprise after the first wash. Fabrics most likely to shrink are made of 100% cotton. If you buy a very long piece of fabric [more than three metres or yards], don't wash it in one piece because it will get twisted and tangled into a discouraging mess in washer and dryer. Instead, cut a piece long enough for a garment, measure it carefully in both length and width, and wash and dry it. If it doesn't shrink, you don't need to wash the rest [unless dirty or pressed off-grain]. If it shrinks, cut the rest into pieces of two to three metres or yards each, and preshrink them too. Another smart way to preshrink a long piece of fabric is to fold it neatly [accordion style] into a bathtub full of water, soak it thoroughly and let it drip-dry over a wooden rod extended over the tub. Iron if necessary prior to cutting it out to recapture that store-bought crispness.

If you buy stretch fabric knitted into a tube without selvages [or with selvages sewn together], preshrink it that way to prevent the edges from curling. If you preshrink fabrics that ravel easily, zigzag or overlock all cut edges first.

Sometimes you can make beautiful clothes for children out of grownups' old clothes for literally no cost. Your old T-shirts can have a beautiful comeback turned into tiny garments. Men's old undershirts, soft and lintfree from repeated washings, would be just perfect for infants' underwear. Don't bother undoing old seams, just cut them off. Check both right and wrong side of fabric and use the better one. Many of my readers write that they buy second-hand clothes for pennies from garage sales to transform into new garments. That is a wonderful way of recycling our resources. Also rescue all good buttons, belt buckles and zippers from discarded garments. It is even fashionable to go back to basics, to stop wasting, and to do anything with your hands, so you can proudly brag about your creative ideas and savings to your envious friends! Better yet, get together to share ideas, to sew, and to have a good time.

I have dozens of bargain fabrics at home. When the inspiration hits me, I cut out several garments one day and sew them the next. It's just like preparing many dishes at the same time for the freezer. When you buy fabrics that you don't use right away, don't hide them in bags in lost places to be forgotten. Fold them neatly on a closet shelf or in a drawer where they are easily accessible and visible to inspire you. Stop feeling guilty about all those bargain fabrics accumulating in your sewing corner! Don't feel you must sew them into something right away. "Fabric addiction" is quite enjoyable and harmless and you are entitled to a few "collection errors" on your way to creative sewing.

My favorite fabrics are 100% cottons (including corduroy, Indian cotton, seersucker, eyelet, batiste, etc.), cotton knits (unfortunately hard to find so I often have to settle for cotton-polyester blends), stretch terry, velour, fleece (woven or sweatshirt fabrics), and quilted fabrics. They are easy-care, wash-and-wear type fabrics, easy to sew, comfortable to wear, and they look nice. For adult clothes, I also use silk types, crepe de chine, wool flannel, jersey, and fine wool or blends. Flame-retardant fabrics are required by law on children's sleepwear.

THREAD

Thread is as important as the fabric. It's false economy to use poor quality thread. It may break when sewing and washing because it is not strong enough. It may have knots and snags or it may not be colorfast. Use good quality thread and, if you have not yet tried cotton wrapped polyester thread, you are in for a pleasant surprise. It has combined the good qualities of both cotton and polyester and sews smoothly with tanglefree, slightly stretchy results.

I keep a supply of basic colors on hand so I don't have to rush to the store just for thread every time I feel like sewing.

For best results and correct tension, use the same thread both in the needle and bobbin. Polyester thread frays easily when broken. It should, therefore, be cut with scissors on a slant so it will be easier to thread the needle.

Does your upper thread often get wound up around the spool-holder underneath the spool? So annoying! Prevent it by sewing a simple tube from cotton knit or rib knit. Make the tube as high as the spool and loose enough so that the spool can turn easily inside it. With slit rim of spool at bottom (so thread doesn't get caught in the slit), slip the tube around the spool with thread running from the top. This tube will save you much frustration and is reusable for all the spools of same size. While you are at it, make a few extras as gifts for friends.

MACHINE NEEDLES

Change blunt or bent machine needles immediately and, for all stretch fabrics, use ballpoint needles or universal point needles. The universal point needle is practical for "lazy sewers" since it can be used on both knits and wovens. Regular needles break stretchy fibers and cause holes and runs. Change the needle to a smaller size when sewing lightweight fabrics.

Machine needles should be replaced frequently when sewing synthetic fabrics because synthetic fibers are more abrasive than natural fibers and dull the needle rapidly. Dull needles may cause bad or skipped stitches, puckered seams, thread breakage, tangling of thread and small tears in fiber, causing runs. Although the cause may be elsewhere, try changing the needle first if you have any of those problems.

PINS

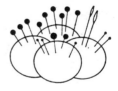

Have a good supply of rustfree, sharp pins. I love extra-long pins with large colored balls. They are designed for knits and thick fabrics, but I use them for practically everything. Basting is time consuming so save it for complicated designs that must be fitted. For the easy designs in this book, with a little practice, pins work just as well. Pin the seams conveniently crosswise with the pin heads to the right, so you can pull the pins out without stopping the machine just before the presser foot starts sliding over the pin. If you use smaller pins and fairly long stitches and have a "hinged" presser foot, you can also stitch right across pins, but I would not recommend it since it may dull the machine needle quickly. For short seams, it is easy to sew not only without basting but without pins as well.

SCISSORS

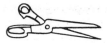

Buy the best quality steel scissors and you'll enjoy them for years to come. Remember, you are saving so much money by sewing that you deserve the best tools you can buy. Spread the word that good sewing tools make excellent gifts.

You will need a large pair for cutting out fabrics, and small ones for snipping thread ends and trimming seams. Have your scissors sharpened regularly. For smooth cutting without creaking, squeeze a drop of machine oil into the screw where the blades cross as soon as you buy the scissors, and once or twice a year thereafter.

To keep your sewing scissors sharp for a long time, use them only for fabrics. Have another pair for cutting out paper.

BUTTONS, ZIPPERS, ETC.

If you have to drive to a store just to buy a set of buttons, they may end up costing more than the fabric, besides taking too much time. I bought a two-pound bag of hundreds of assorted buttons years ago for a dollar, and have been using them for countless garments, especially for children's clothes. As a bonus, my son played with them for years, sorting the buttons out by color and size, counting them and "goldmining" the prettiest ones. I almost did not buy that bag for those unusual, crazy and glimmering buttons, because I thought I could not possibly use them for anything. For a child with a healthy dose of imagination, they are gold nuggets and diamonds. Now that my little daughter is old enough not to put the buttons in her mouth, my collection is inspiring her, too, in many happy games while I am sewing. Not bad for an inexpensive bag of buttons! I now keep refilling my button box from time to time.

Whenever there is a sale particularly a clearance sale, I buy zippers, bias tape, ribbons, wide elastic, appliqués, or whatever I happen to find at a real bargain-price for future use. Sometimes a large, beautiful zipper with an interesting, decorative tab inspires me to create a whole garment around it.

Regard sewing the same way as you do cooking. You need staples at home to be creative any time you get an inspiration.

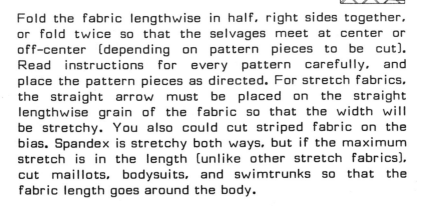

CUTTING THE FABRIC

Fold the fabric lengthwise in half, right sides together, or fold twice so that the selvages meet at center or off-center (depending on pattern pieces to be cut). Read instructions for every pattern carefully, and place the pattern pieces as directed. For stretch fabrics, the straight arrow must be placed on the straight lengthwise grain of the fabric so that the width will be stretchy. You also could cut striped fabric on the bias. Spandex is stretchy both ways, but if the maximum stretch is in the length (unlike other stretch fabrics), cut maillots, bodysuits, and swimtrunks so that the fabric length goes around the body.

It is very important to cut the fabric out on the straight grain, because otherwise the garment will appear twisted. As mentioned earlier, dampen the fabric to straighten the grainline, pull on the bias and press, if necessary.

Many stretch fabrics tend to curl around cut edges. It is annoying to stitch such edges together. You can partly eliminate this problem by handling the cut edges as little as possible, and avoid pulling and stretching them after cutting. Use lots of pins (or good old basting) to straighten the curly edges prior to sewing.

Pin the pattern pieces on folded fabric. Mark the cutting lines with tailor's chalk. With a little practice, you can skip marking the cutting line and simply cut directly along the pattern edge. Instead of pins, you can use some weights (such as books or canned foods) to hold the pattern pieces in place.

When cutting out fabrics with one-way nap (such as velour, terry, corduroy, velvet, velveteen), be sure to have the nap running downward for every pattern piece, for a smooth touch and even color. Otherwise it will look as if you have cut the pattern pieces from two different shades. I have seen many commercial patterns and sewing books instruct you to cut the nap upward for deeper shade. However, I have always regretted cutting the fabric that way because it felt rough and unpleasant to touch.

Test if knit fabric runs and if so, in which direction. It is wise to cut the pattern so that it will run upwards from where there is less pressure on garment (such as hemline instead of shoulders, or sleeve ends instead of sleeve tops).

Follow grainline indications on the pattern pieces carefully, especially when cutting stretch fabrics. Remember that the stretchy crosswise grain must almost always go around the body (or perhaps cut on the bias for striped knits), not up and down. Occasionally the fabric is sufficiently stretchy in both length and width, and then it is possible to cut the pattern either way, providing that the fabric hangs properly both ways.

Place pattern pieces that are so directed on fold and cut only the cutting lines. When you need to cut two identical but asymmetric pieces (front-halfs, raglan sleeves, kangaroo pockets), cut the pattern out of double-layered fabric, so the pieces will automatically be mirror images of each other. When you need only one piece and not on the fold, open up the fabric prior to cutting. Sometimes you save fabric by not folding it exactly in half, so it is wise to plan the layout carefully for all pieces prior to cutting.

To save time and pattern paper, I have drawn only half of most patterns, even sleeves, that have identical other halves. However, if you want a complete sleeve pattern, enlarge the half-sleeve as shown onto folded pattern paper. When back and front are identical except for neckline, I have drawn them as one so you need to enlarge only one pattern piece instead of two. First cut two back pieces on fabric fold, remove one of them as the final back piece, and cut lower neckline for front as shown. Some patterns have identical front and back except for neckline and center front, such as jacket or coat. Enlarge the pattern with all lines as shown, cut out one back piece on fold, and then use the same pattern to cut out the two front sections along selvages of the fabric.

SEWING STRETCHY

Stretch fabrics are easy to sew, they fit well, don't show wrinkles, and they give neat results with a little experience and know-how. You don't need to leave much ease for action and comfort since the stretchy ease is built right into the fabric itself.

Whenever you sew stretch fabrics, use a ballpoint or universal point needle, polyester or cotton-wrapped polyester thread, and stretch stitch (or overlock, quick seam, or tiny zigzag). If your machine only has a straight stitch, you must stretch the fabric as you sew and stitch the seams twice.

Improvised quick seam: One version of "quick seam" can be sewn with the same stitch that you would use for blind hem stitch. So, even if your sewing machine manual doesn't tell you that, you can use the blind hem stitch as a quick seam for lightweight stretch fabrics. Keep the raw edges to the left (unlike most other sewing), adjust the stitch width to the widest, and the stitch length as short as desired.

Use shortcuts whenever possible in cutting and sewing, but it is worth it to take extra time to topstitch neatly and to match stripes and plaids for perfect results. I like topstitching with a double needle for facings around neck openings, sleeve ends, hems, and pockets. A double needle gives professional and neat results so easily.

ELASTICS

Elastics are practical and easy to apply when you know a few tips for neat and comfortable results. Elastic should never be too tight because restricting blood circulation is both harmful and painful.

Self-casing: Use this method when you don't use topstitched elastic (described later) for shorts, pull-on pants, pull-on skirt waist, sleeve and leg ends. Overlock the raw edge of fabric and press it to inside, stitch close to raw edge forming a casing and leaving an opening for elastic. Cut elastic the desired length and insert it through the casing with safety pin or bodkin. Make sure the elastic is not twisted (it's helpful to mark both ends of "right side" prior to inserting the elastic through the casing). Join the ends without overlapping and stitch them together securely by machine or hand. Don't use a knot to tie the ends together. Stitch opening closed. To prevent elastic from rolling, stitch elastic along seams (stitch-in-ditch) through all thicknesses. These stitches will not be visible. (Sew casing around neck opening with facing or extra-wide bias tape.)

Elasticized waistline with or without casing: When elasticizing the waistline, use one of the following methods:

A) If there is a seam (such as joining bodice to skirt or romper top to shorts), stitch stretched elastic directly to seam allowance on the wrong side of garment.

B) If there is no seam at waist, try the garment on, and tie elastic around waist. Pull the fabric above the elastic until desired fullness is achieved. Clearly mark this line as the waistline by running a basting thread along the lower side of elastic, so you will be able to see it on the wrong side. (Do this prior to hemming the lower edge, because elasticizing the waistline will shorten the garment.) Turn the garment inside out. Zigzag stretched elastic along marked line, dividing the fullness evenly between equal sections of elastic and fabric.

C) Elastic through casing. Mark the waistline as above. Stitch a fabric strip or bias tape to the wrong side of garment along marked waistline, stitching both upper and lower edges to form a casing and leaving an opening. Insert elastic through opening and stitch elastic ends together. Stitch opening closed. Divide fullness evenly at front and back. Stitch elastic along side seams through all thicknesses to prevent it from rolling.

Topstitched elastic: This is a neat, fast and twistproof way to elasticize cut edges of waist, leg and sleeve ends, and neck opening of any garment, even swimwear. Cut elastic the desired length and, without overlapping, zigzag ends together into a circle. Divide both elastic and fabric edge into equal sections by using pins or by marking with tailor's chalk. Fabric edge even with elastic edge, zigzag elastic to the wrong side of garment. Stretch each section of elastic as needed while you sew so the garment edge lies flat. For a narrow elastic, stitch top edge only. For a wider elastic, stitch both edges. As you stitch, hold elastic taut both in front of and behind the presser foot. Turn the elasticized edge to the inside, and edgestitch from wrong side, stretching the elastic as you sew so that fabric lies flat. If desired, stitch additional rows through elastic from right side, stretching while you sew.

Depending on the width and quality of elastic and fabric used, and especially if additional topstitched rows are added, elastic ribbon will stretch when stitched through as described above. Since this type of elasticized edge is very bothersome to undo, test first on a scrap fabric with a short piece of elastic to see the results (and to get used to this method) and adjust the elastic length for the garment accordingly.

Elastic shirring by machine: If your machine has a special presser foot with a hole in it (for shirring by covering elastic thread with zigzag), follow instructions in your sewing machine manual.

Or use the following easy method. Hand-wind elastic thread around bobbin, stretching slightly. Use polyester or cotton-wrapped polyester thread (not 100% cotton) as upper thread. Stitch from the right side of garment, so the elastic bobbin thread is on the wrong side. Use long machine stitches. Test first on scrap. To mark the first row fast, fold the fabric, press forming a crease, open it up and stitch along the crease. (Or stitch first row so that the side of presser foot runs along fabric edge which has been cut on selvage or narrowly hemmed or trimmed with lace.) When stitching additional rows, hold the fabric taut both in front of and behind the presser foot. Make each row of elastic stitching so that the previous row runs along the side of presser foot. Be sure to lock each stitching line securely at the beginning and end with backward stitches (or knot thread ends securely together).

Before sewing with elastic thread, check it first to see if it is of good quality. Stretch the thread to its maximum length. If it breaks easily, return the thread to the store for an exchange. Although bad quality is quite unusual, I mention it because I once wasted hours trying to figure out what I was doing wrong.

Shirring with elastic thread in the bobbin may loosen the bobbin thread tension. If that happens, you'll have to tighten the tension afterward before sewing with regular thread again. Simply tighten the screw in the bobbin case until you get proper tension, or follow directions in your sewing machine manual.

Depending on fabric and stitch length, elastic shirring will shorten the original length of fabric (i.e. the direction in which you are sewing, whether it is along shoulder straps or around body) to about half. Therefore, if you wish to add elastic shirring to pattern pieces that are not designed for that, shirring is best done prior to cutting out the fabric.

BIAS TAPES
AND STRETCH TAPES

Bias tapes and stretch tapes are useful for binding raw edges neatly and quickly.

<u>Bias tape</u> is a strip of non-stretch fabric cut on the bias.

<u>Stretch tape</u> is a strip of stretch fabric cut across the width. It is not necessary to cut stretch fabric on the bias. Cutting across the stretchy width is more convenient and usually saves fabric too. (Exception: When binding raw edges of a stretch garment that don't have to stretch, you might find it more practical and neater to cut the strips lengthwise along non-stretchy grain.)

Ready-made, prefolded bias tape is inexpensive and available in practically any color. However, since it is made from non-stretch fabric, I find it too stiff for soft, lightweight, or stretch garments. It is easy to make your own tape from the same fabric as the garment. Or use a different fabric (such as rib knit strips) or contrasting color for a beautiful decorative effect.

Commercial bias tape is known as singlefold or doublefold. In this book I use mainly self-made tapes folded differently from store-bought ones so I use the following terms (all explained below): unifold, bifold, trifold. (Trifold tape is commercially known as doublefold.)

Making bias tapes

Cut strips of non-stretch fabric on the bias. Depending on use, press the strips unifold, bifold or trifold as explained below for stretch tapes.

Making unifold stretch tape

Cut a strip 2cm (3/4") wide (or twice the desired finished width) across the width of stretch fabric. Wrong sides in, press the strip in half lengthwise. Bind raw fabric edge with the prepared tape. Topstitch the tape in place with short but wide zigzag which will cover raw tape edges for neat and unbulky results. Unifold stretch tape is soft and pliable so it's suitable especially for children's clothes and just perfect for cotton knits, stretch terry and velour.

Making bifold stretch tape

This is a practical way to avoid bulk when sewing velour or terry (or when using bulky fabrics to make bias tapes such as corduroy). Under the fabric it will look like unifold tape, and on the top like trifold tape. Cut a strip 4½cm (1 3/4") wide (or three times the desired finished width) across the width of stretch fabric. Press one-third of width under, then press the entire strip in half lengthwise wrong sides in, so that raw edge and folded edge meet. Cleanfinish the outer raw edge with overlock. Bind raw fabric edge with the prepared tape so that the tape's folded edge is on the right side of garment. Topstitch through all thicknesses.

Making trifold stretch tape (Commercially known as doublefold)

Cut a strip 5cm (2") wide (or four times the desired

finished width) across the width of stretch fabric. Wrong sides in, press the strip in half lengthwise (to mark the center line), open it up and press both long edges to center of strip, then press the entire strip refolded on center line again. Bind raw fabric edge with the prepared tape. Topstitch it in place through all thicknesses with straight stitch, zigzag or decorative stitch. Or stitch it in place in two steps: First stitch the underseam by holding the opened-up tape under the garment, raw edges together and right side of tape against wrong side of fabric, stitching on the first fold. Now turn the tape over the edge to the right side, so that tape's center fold is binding the raw fabric edge, and the unstitched folded side of tape covers the first stitching line. Topstitch through all thicknesses. Use any stitch but, if around pullover's small neckhole, use only stretch stitch for sufficient ease and stretch.

RIB KNIT BANDS

Rib knit fabric is available by the metre (or yard) in a variety of widths and weights, and in different colors. Cut it into close-fitting bands for neck opening, waist, wrists, and ankles of T-shirts, playsuits, pajamas and sportswear. Rib knit bands are also used for garments made of non-stretch fabrics as wristbands, waistbands and neckbands. Rib knit can also be purchased in packaged quantities (called "ribbing") cut and finished to a specific length and width.

Unfortunately, rib knit fabric is not available in every fabric store. Keep asking for it and eventually the situation should improve now that it is becoming so popular. When I find rib knit fabric in inexpensive stores, I buy several colors in quantity. Some old knit sweaters or T-shirts might be used for rib knit bands. I have even bought a few new stretch nylon pullovers at sales, to cut into rib knit bands. Don't throw away old socks and kneehighs because usually only the sole is worn. Stretchy ankles and legs make excellent ribbing for sleeve and leg ends on children's T-shirts, pajamas and sportswear. The upper edge is non-raveling and doesn't even have to be folded. If the right side is worn and linty, check to see if the wrong side looks better. Before discarding old garments, check for any rib knit cuffs or waistbands in good shape for new use. If you can't find rib knit fabrics in stores, ask for any very stretchy fabric and you might find a good substitute.

To prepare a rib knit band to be sewn to the garment, cut a strip twice the desired finished length (here referring to the lengthwise grain) plus seam allowances, and as wide as desired (here referring to the stretchy crosswise grain) plus seam allowances. For a neat fit, the rib knit band is always cut somewhat shorter than the length of edge it is sewn to. Stitch band ends together from wrong side, forming a tube. Then fold the band in half (across stretchy width), wrong sides in and raw edges even (press lightly, if necessary, but without stretching the band). For a neckband or waistband, divide both the band and the garment's edge into four (or eight) equal sections and mark them with pins or tailor's chalk. It's not necessary to divide short edges such as cuffs or legbands. <u>Turn the garment inside out including sleeve ends and leg ends.</u> This is an easy and neat way to stitch rib knit bands around even the smallest sleeve ends (you don't put the sleeve ends around freearm). Pin the band inside (against the right side of garment), all raw edges even, matching marks. Place the band seam at neck center back, or at side seam of sleeves, legs, and waist. Rib knit band up against the presser foot and all raw edges even, stitch the band in place, stretching it as needed to straighten the garment's edge. Do not stretch the garment. Sew as you would sew any stretch fabric, i.e. by using ballpoint needle, polyester thread, and stretch stitch (or overlock or tiny zigzag).

When using a rib knit band around neck with front opening (jacket, coat), press the band in half right side out. Taper the front ends into rounded corners by pulling them down and cutting off the excess seam allowances. Band against the right side of garment and all raw edges even, pin the band around the neck and stitch it in place.

When sewing a rib knit band around the lower edge of a jacket with front opening, sew the band in place prior to stitching the zipper (sewing the zipper in place will close the band ends). If using buttons or snap fasteners instead of zipper closure, stitch band ends closed from wrong side prior to sewing the band around the lower edge of garment.

Instead of using rib knit fabric, you can make bands from self-fabric of a stretchy garment, or even from a different stretch fabric (maybe of contrasting color). Prepare the band and stitch it in place as described above. Neckband should be large enough, when stretched, for the head to fit through but not too large or it will look droopy. Generally speaking, you will not get as close-fitting bands from regular stretch fabrics as you will from rib knit, which combines stretch and close fit for a professional, neat look.

The seam joining the neckband to a stretch fabric T-shirt or pullover must be stretchy. If you only have a straight stitch machine and you wish to sew stretch fabrics, stitch the seam twice and stretch the fabric slightly as you sew. Add an opening with zipper, or button and loop, to the back of close-fitting, round neck opening, or choose a model with boat neck or V-neck.

Apart from rib knit bands, you can easily make many useful and comfortably warm items out of rib knit fabrics. Consider making tuques, balaclava helmets, tubular hoods (long enough to drape around neck), legwarmers, tank tops, extra-long wrists for mittens (to pull them over snowsuit sleeves), and sporty headbands. Use rib knit also for store-bought garments. Let's say you bought a nylon windbreaker for a child, and in no time it is too short. Cut off elasticized sleeve ends and cordstring casing from around the lower edge and extend the hem and sleeve ends with rib knit bands. If a hood is too loose or doesn't cover the forehead, sew a rib knit band around hood front edge, forming a casing, and insert a cord through it.

DECORATING GARMENTS WITH SEWING MACHINE

Decorating garments with your sewing machine can be fun and easy. This chapter gives you smart Ideas on machine appliqués, machine embroidery, monograms and machine quilting, and on camouflaging accidents.

Use these methods to decorate children's clothes such as T-shirts, sweatshirts, vests, jackets, bibs and pockets of overalls and jumpers. Decorate adult garments of simple designs such as vests, jackets, capes, sweatshirts, T-shirts and kimonos. Garment sections are most conveniently decorated before stitching the seams.

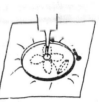

For professional results, loosen the top tension slightly to ensure that bobbin thread or links will not be visible on the right side of garment. Lock the stitching lines at the beginning and end with a few straight stitches while the stitch length is in zero position.

When you have time and you are in a creative mood, make several appliqués for future use (by using "Ready-sewn method" described later). Then, when you need an appliqué, it will be a pleasure to select one from your stock and stitch it to the garment.

Make your own appliqués with either of these two easy methods ["Ready-sewn method" and "Fusing method"]. After a little practice, they'll look just as good as store-bought ones.

Choosing the design and material for appliqués: Simple, bold designs are best. Trace patterns from magazines or children's books, or make your own. Experiment with a variety of fabric scraps with interesting textures such as Ultrasuede, velour, spandex, nylon, quilted fabrics, lace, lamés and sparkling fabrics, velveteen, fake fur, as well as regular cotton and polyester. Tightly woven fabrics are best. Add stability and body, if necessary, to limp or loosely-woven fabrics by ironing fusible interfacing to wrong side of appliqué materials. Remember that appliqué will be washed along with the garment so choose the material accordingly [preshrink if necessary].

Ready-sewn method: This method is practical and neat for appliqués consisting of one piece, or of separate pieces that are joined together or partially overlapped. You satin stitch the raw edges of the appliqué and add the details until the appliqué is completely finished, and only then do you stitch it to the garment. Cut the appliqué piece(s) out of desired fabric(s). Choose color(s) in contrast to the garment. If the design consists of several pieces, iron fusible interfacing to the wrong side to join the separate pieces together. Place a sheet of typing paper [or tear-away stabilizer such as Pellon] under the appliqué. Use embroidery foot. Cover all raw edges with satin stitch [wide, short zigzag]. The typing paper [or tear-away stabilizer] helps you to stitch neatly

around edges and keeps the appliqué flat. Rip the paper (or stabilizer) off after you have finished sewing. Press the finished appliqué with steam iron. Stitch it to the garment with regular straight stitch (stitching along the inner edge of satin stitch will be least visible).

Fusing method: This method is convenient for large appliqués, or for appliqués with several non-joined pieces. Cut the appliqué piece(s) out of desired fabric(s). Bond the piece(s) to the garment by ironing with strips of fusible web between the appliqué and the garment. Place a sheet of typing paper (or tear-away stabilizer) underneath (between the garment and feed dogs), tear off after sewing. Use embroidery foot. Cover all raw edges of appliqué with satin stitch. Press.

Monograms: When sewing a monogram, trace the letter (or number) onto the fabric. For soft or stretch fabric, iron a piece of interfacing underneath, or slip a sheet of typing paper under the fabric. Use an embroidery hoop to keep fabric straight and taut (larger hoop on wrong side of work). Stitch the monogram with wide zigzag by dropping the feed control. Use darning foot and guide the work by hand without turning the fabric. Remember to lower the presser foot. Sew fast but move the hoop slowly so zigzag stitches will be very close together. Move the hoop faster when moving sideways. The finished monogram should be smooth and even. If it has gaps, sew a second run over the first one. Press with steam iron.

Monogramming is like writing with the needle. Experiment first on scrap fabric.

If your machine doesn't have a dropfeed control, use embroidery foot and stitch the monogram with regular satin stitch (sewing forward only), turning the fabric to follow the monogram lines.

To monogram fabric with nap or pile (such as corduroy, velour or terry) that wouldn't show tracing, trace the monogram on a sheet of typing paper. Position the fabric (with the paper on top) over the larger hoop and snap in the smaller ring (to keep both the fabric and the paper straight and taut). Stitch the monogram as above and tear the paper off after you have finished. Or, instead of paper, trace the design (backward) onto the wrong side of fabric, and hand-baste along the lines so that they show on right side.

Monogram garment prior to stitching the seams. Small items, such as a pocket, should be monogrammed prior to cutting the fabric. If you decide to monogram a pocket after you have already cut it out, baste pocket securely onto a larger piece of scrap fabric to enable you to use a hoop (trim excess scrap fabric off after you have finished).

Machine embroidery (outline method):
This easy method gives a beautiful decorative effect on a garment of a solid color. Use a drawing from a magazine or draw your own design on a sheet of paper, but don't cut it out. Iron interfacing under the fabric (or slip a sheet of typing paper or tear-away stabilizer underneath; rip it off after you have finished). Baste the entire drawing onto the garment with several vertical and horizontal lines to keep it securely in place. Use embroidery foot. Satin stitch all the lines of the drawing

with short, wide zigzag, using contrasting colored thread(s). After you have finished, rip off the drawing which is now broken where stitched through. The traces of paper left under stitches will wash away. Or, instead of satin stitch, stitch the drawing lines and details with free-motion straight stitch by dropping the feed dogs.

Machine embroidery (filling method):

Fill the above-mentioned outlined drawing entirely with free-motion zigzag or straight stitch in different colors. It's as if you would be darning a hole or, let's say, painting a picture. And, by the way, it is a smart way to camouflage a tear or hole. Use a darning foot (or no foot). Lower the feed dogs so you will be able to guide the fabric by hand in any direction (even backwards). Lower the presser foot lever. Before you start sewing, hold the thread ends taut to the back so they won't get drawn into the needleplate hole. Consider embroidering a nice design on a pocket, the bib of a child's jumpsuit or chef's apron, or on a kimono back.

Decorative satin stitch: To decorate
garments, you don't even need to use any specific design. Just a plain satin stitch in contrasting color forming a few stripes, curves, or whatever, across pockets, sleeve ends or bodice gives the garment that special, unique touch. No dropfeed control is necessary for this type of machine embroidery.

Machine quilting: This gives a lovely
touch to a garment. Quilt prior to sewing the seams. Baste a layer of quilt batting (or a layer or two of fleece or cotton knit fabric) between two layers of garment fabric (cut pattern parts to be quilted

double-layered). Topstitch multiple rows of straight or curvy lines (or "draw" a design with the machine needle) through all thicknesses.

For a repeat pattern (such as straight or curvy lines spaced at equal distance), make a template from self-adhesive vinyl; peel off the paper, stick vinyl onto fabric and stitch along (not through) edges; pull vinyl off and stick it in next position.

Quilting is suitable for garment parts that don't need to stretch. Use it for yokes, cuffs, belts, waistbands, neckbands of front-open jackets or V-neck pullovers. Consider this method also for decorating small parts of bodice front or back or sleeves of T-shirts, sweatshirts, dresses and jackets. Cut entire pockets double-layered for this purpose. Machine quilting looks good in velour, fleece, terry, cotton, nylon and silky fabrics.

Camouflage mistakes: Do it by something so smart it makes the accident a lucky one. I once burned the hem of a minidress, and covered the burn with patch pockets (decoratively topstitched) at the hemline. Sure enough, it was just the pockets, so unusually placed and decorated, that everyone admired. When a friend of mine mistakenly cut a blouse too narrow, she added a wide lace inset to side and underarm seams, and that made the blouse even more beautiful than the original design. Another friend burned the sleeve ends of a sheer blouse and covered the burns cleverly with rows of satin ribbons.

Let your own accidents challenge you to find perfect solutions to camouflage them!

SEWING IS MY HOBBY

I inherited my interest in sewing from my mother. It is thanks to her encouragement during my childhood in Finland that, for more than three decades now, I have found sewing to be such a source of pleasure, as well as an easy and enjoyable way of being creative. At times, sewing has even been an economical necessity.

Always interested in sewing or, let's say, easy sewing, I have tried to find shortcuts for quick yet beautiful results ever since I was six years old. My first attempts were disastrous. I reasoned that since dolls don't move, I could just as well baste the seams together and whip up a dozen garments, while my older sister labored with tiny stitches on the only dress she was able to finish in the meantime. I thought I was very smart -- until I tried dressing the dolls. All my beautiful creations fell apart. With that I learned the first important lesson in the art of sewing.

I still remember vividly how impressed I was to see my mother cut out a pair of panties for my doll without a pattern. Without realizing it then, I started storing in my mind the basics of pattern-making. My parents were farmers and we lived in the country far away from any good shopping facilities. Even if patterns had existed, country women found it more practical to make their own and share them with each other. The upper part of patterns were cut out of newspapers or brown wrapping paper "with a little short bit of upper bodice and a little short bit of upper sleeve" as my mother used to say. She used to draw the rest of the pattern herself according to the child's measurements.

That indeed was the only way of home sewing in the country because, back in the early 50's, commercial patterns for children were unavailable. I have three sisters, so it was practical to make dresses for all of us at the same time by just altering the pattern size slightly for each one. She encouraged us to use the sewing machine and bought lots of inexpensive fabrics so we could practice. I was ten years old when I made my first dress without a pattern. I can still remember how pretty it was when I wore it to school. That is how I got happily hooked on sewing.

I mention these early experiences in the hope that sewing mothers everywhere would share their talent with their children, to "teach them something worthwhile", as one of my readers so nicely put it. Encouragement does not mean proving how much better you are, but being there with a helping hand and lots of compliments. Many patterns in this book are so simple that even a ten year old child could sew them (perhaps with a little help from you).

At 15, I started sewing regularly and, due to my mother's style of sewing, it was natural to make my own patterns, although I used commercial patterns too. I now realize the talent and the patience my mother had, as well as the value of her teaching to last me a lifetime. Even if you didn't learn sewing from your own mother and have not had much experience in sewing, it is never too late to start. I hope this book will encourage you to realize that anyone can easily learn how to sew.

I have learned a lot since those early childhood days. Today sewing is my number one hobby, and for a good reason. While it saves money, it is also a rewarding occupation which gives quick results that can actually be worn immediately and get envious compliments from others. Unbelievable as it may sound, sewing can save time too. Just think of all the time spent shopping for ready-made clothes (often at rush-hour with tired children), trying them on, being frustrated by prices, shrinking garments, fixing poorly-made seams or rescuing loose buttons in time. At home, you can sew in comfort at any convenient time with this selection of basic patterns and an easy method of drawing new ones when necessary. Of course my sewing is now more than just a hobby since my dearest occupation has turned into the business that I subconsciously always wanted.

In these days sewing is easy and enjoyable thanks to good sewing machines, beautiful easy-care fabrics, and innumerable time-saving gadgets and notions to smooth away many frustrations.

Sewing for children can truly be a pleasure. It is very economical, not too complicated, it gives you a chance to be creative and use your imagination, and provides valuable experience for more serious and more complicated sewing projects. Furthermore, self-made children's clothes make wonderful gifts. I make most of my children's clothes at a savings of 60-90% as compared to ready-made clothing.

As a bonus, sewing keeps the children happily busy. They love the creative atmosphere around your sewing machine, and will be inspired to invent their own games to the theme. Children are resourceful enough to profit from almost any opportunity and will gradually collect many treasures among the empty spools, material scraps, ribbons and pretty buttons.

Still a fan of quick sewing, I am always searching for new ideas on easy and enjoyable shortcuts, while over the years I have developed many of my own. I am happy to share them with you through this book.

CREATE YOUR OWN DESIGNS

This collection of basic patterns provides you with an endless source of versatile, timeless designs, that are simple to sew. Use them as a guide to create your own styles which reflect your personal needs and tastes.

Leaf through all designs and directions and you might find useful tips and ideas in them, even if you don't use some patterns "as is".

Pull-on pants and shorts designed without side seams can be trimmed down sides with contrasting stripes or tapes for a sporty look. Or, for mock cording, place the cord along leg's side-fold on wrong side of fabric. Fold fabric over cord and topstitch from the right side through both thicknesses with zipper foot close to covered cord, encasing it tightly. Or, cut the pattern apart at sides from waist to hem, add seam allowances, and stitch piping (from bias tape) between seams.

I have mentioned variations for some of these patterns. Pull-on pants with sweatshirt can be unisex pajamas or sportswear. Cut a T-shirt longer for a dress or nightgown. A jacket can also become a coat or bathrobe. With a pattern for pull-on pants, cutting lines allow you to make shorts too.

Once you get used to it, it is easier to manipulate a miniature pattern than a full-size one. Try changing my patterns or designing a few of your own on any paper with small squares. Once it "looks" right, enlarge it (recheck the measurements at this point before cutting out the fabric) and sew it, and you might well have discovered a rewarding, hidden talent that will continue to give you creative pleasure in the future.

An easy way to start designing your own patterns is to use a basic pattern as a guide, and add your own touch to it. Take a sleeveless top and add a gathered ruffle from self-fabric or different fabric to make a lovely summer dress. Take a maillot, make it a bodysuit, add sleeves if desired, add a little ruffled skirt below waist, and make it a skating or gym suit. Take a T-shirt, add a ruffle or ruffled lace between sleeves and bodice and lengthen it for a nightgown. Or take a simple, favorite garment such as a T-shirt or pajamas that your child has outgrown, and try making a pattern from it, lengthening it at the same time. You don't even need to cut the original garment apart to make a pattern. Just place the old garment, appropriately folded, directly onto the fabric, add some extra plus seam allowances, and cut it out. Or, measure the old garment for all necessary measurements, add some extra plus seam allowances, and draw a new pattern.

Once you have enlarged a pattern, let it inspire you to create a unique, new design. Cut it apart any way you like, vertically, horizontally or on the bias. Add seam allowances to all newly-made seams. Cut the separate pieces out of complimentary colors, or out of different fabrics, or add piping trim in between. This is especially easy and attractive for T-shirts and sweatshirts, maillots and swimtrunks.

Start your own fashion scrapbook. Whenever you see something you like in magazine articles and advertisements, at stores, or on TV, cut it out or make a simple sketch so you won't forget it. Then go through the patterns in this book to see if any of them could be used "as is", enlarged or reduced, combined, or adapted to sew that garment.

Good ideas are there all around you. All you have to do is to realize that you can easily create the same or even better designs and sew them yourself. You will be so happy and proud of yourself, that you might want to order some labels (original by...) to attach to garments you have sewn. You'll find such labels by mail-order advertised in sewing magazines or they can be ordered through some fabric stores.

EASY WEAR AND CARE

Everyday clothes for children should be made with easy-care fabrics, so they can be machine washed and dried. These clothes must withstand repeated washings and should be easy to put on and take off.

To encourage children to dress themselves, mark the back of pull-on pants, T-shirts, sweatshirts, and pull-on skirts [when the back and front are so similar that it is difficult to tell them apart] with a piece of ribbon, tape or yarn stitched to the inside of waistband or neckband.

When using a drawstring cord through waist or hood casing, prevent it from slipping out by catching the cord to the casing at waist center back and hood center top with a few stitches. This is a practical tip also for store-bought garments.

To add extra strength to garments sewn with straight stitch, stitch seams like crotch and armholes twice. Stretch stitch is more durable than straight stitch, so double stitching is not necessary. Sew buttons very securely with buttonhole twist thread or dental floss. Use fusible web for quick hems if you don't use topstitching, which usually is the fastest and the most durable way to hem children's clothes. Add patches to pants' knees prior to sewing side seams. Cut the patches as wide as the pants, stitch upper and lower edges securely to the wrong side of the garment, and stitch patch sides together with side seams and inner leg seams.

When washing garments, close all zippers, open buttons and empty pockets [brush them out if necessary]. To keep them looking great longer, all garments [but especially those made of fabrics with nap, such as velour and corduroy] should be turned inside out. That way they don't spread their lint to other items in the wash, or attract lint from other items that may stick to their nap.

Today's easy-care fabrics and lifestyle almost prohibit the use of an iron. However, a good steam iron nowadays is so light and easy to use, and gives such a lovely, almost luxurious feeling to clothes that, from time to time, I find myself actually enjoying a little ironing just to touch up. Perhaps the beautiful smell of clean, freshly ironed laundry brings back nostalgic childhood memories that I want to pass on to my own children.

SEWING FOR ALLERGIC CHILDREN

If you sew for an allergic child with a sensitive skin, use these tips for comfort.

Neckbands, sleeves and waistbands should not be too tight to cause irritation. Seams should be narrow and neat, not bulky, and the design should have sufficient ease for free, unrestricted movements. Elastic should be encased and of soft, non-binding quality, and never too tight. Design clothes without zippers or so that the metal part of zipper will not touch the skin.

Synthetic fibers may cause allergic itching. The best fabrics for an allergic child are made of 100% cotton which gets softer and even more comfortable after repeated washings. Excessively warm and thick clothing can cause perspiring, itching and discomfort. An allergic child's clothes (or fabrics prior to sewing) should be washed well, before wearing for the first time, to remove all traces of coloring and finishing agents, that may irritate the skin. Improper rinsing and fabric softeners may also cause irritation for an allergic child.

EXTENDING GARMENT LIFE

Tips for extending garment life are mentioned for some of the designs in this book. Since my style of sewing is so fast and inexpensive, I usually prefer making a brand new garment rather than spending hours on complicated and frustrating alterations to make a garment longer and larger. I have, however, a few favorite, fast tips for extending garment life that you might find useful.

The easiest way to lengthen the dress or skirt, without unstitching the hem, is by stitching a ruffle or eyelet edge around the hem. Or cut all around the hem about 5cm (2") from the lower edge and spread apart by sewing an eyelet or lace insert between.

Pants are designed with straight legs so that, if legs are too long or if you wish to cut them even longer, they are easy and neat just to fold up. (Consider lining lower ends with suitable fabric since they will show when turned up.)

Many of these patterns are designed with raglan or dolman sleeves, or are sleeveless, and made from stretch fabrics for built-in room for growth.

Cut straps for overalls extra long to lengthen them easily by changing the button positions.

If you cut skirts, pants or sleeves with a wide hem allowance to let out later, and the originally folded edge looks faded from wear and washings, conceal it with ribbon or decorative tape or rows of lace, or go over it with permanent marker of matching color.

Cut pull-on pants long enough to use elasticized leg ends. Lengthen the pants later by cutting off the elasticized edges (don't bother undoing the casing) and replacing them with rib knit bands.

For a preschooler, you can use rib knit bands even for overalls and jeans when they become too short. Instead of rib knit, velour works well, too, especially for corduroy pants. The pants will look so smart and will be so warm and convenient with boots, that you can't wait for other pants to get short too. You might even want to cut some pants off just below knees and add long, narrow rib knit bands that extend all the way down to ankles.

You can lengthen overalls or coveralls by cutting the garment apart at waist (rip zipper out temporarily below cut), stitch rib knit or any suitable fabric around waist between the pieces that are cut apart, and stitch lower part of the zipper back in new position. Or make pull-on pants out of them.

52

Add width to garments by stitching decorative fabric strips between side seams, raglan seams, and underarms of sleeve seams.

When you want to make pull-on pants or pull-on skirts out of old garments and don't have enough fabric for self-encased elastic at waist, stitch on decorative wide elastic for a waistband.

When long sleeves become too short, make them short sleeves. A too-short dress can be cut off at underarms to make a skirt with elasticized waist.

When cotton knit pajamas become too short, cut the sleeves and legs shorter. (My son actually prefers them to long pajamas and wants me to sew them short right from the beginning.)

When a coat becomes too short, make it a jacket. Extend sleeves with rib knit bands, cut lower edge at hips and add rib knit waistband.

When a ruffled sundress with shirred upper edge becomes too short, remove the straps and use it as a skirt with shirred upper edge as a waistband.

Certain designs, such as long nightgowns or T-shirtdresses, gradually get shorter while being usable all the time without any effort on your part, the long nightgown becoming a short one, and the T-shirtdress becoming a hip-length blouson and finally a T-shirt.

If a T-shirt is too tight across shoulders, make it a tank top. Cut sleeves off completely, enlarge armholes and neckhole, add doublefold stretch tape or rib knit bands.

If a jacket (corduroy, denim, quilted fabrics) becomes too tight and short, take the sleeves off, and make it a vest. Add rib knit bands to armholes.

Cut jeans short or knee-length, or extend the legs with bands of contrasting fabric (band as wide as the leg ends), and use matching fabric to decorate the jeans with appliqués. You might even like to make a matching vest.

Use the above-mentioned tips also for store-bought clothes. Let every garment inspire you to invent more extension tips to suit the child's needs.

MADE TO MEASURE

Draw your child's outline on a sheet of paper or cardboard, so you can refer to it for sleeve and pants' length, even if the child is sleeping, away, or so squirmy when you sew that you can't try the garment on. Also mention all the important measurements of your child on the paper but remember that children grow very fast and you need new measurements frequently.

If it is impractical to draw the child's outline on a paper, record the measurements at least every six months. A garment of currently suitable size for your child can solve many of your measuring problems when sewing.

PATTERNS

Commercial patterns are well-made with professional and detailed instructions. I have a good collection of them and I subscribe to several home sewing pattern magazines for inspiration and up-to-date fashion information. I have also created my own collection of basic patterns, and have learned to change them for several variations.

When I did not find the patterns I wanted for infants, I made my own. Thereafter, it was natural to continue making patterns for older children and adults too. It can be surprisingly easy, providing you have the time, some patience, and lots of inexpensive fabric for testing. Once you get more experienced in sewing and pattern making, you gain confidence, and will be able to duplicate the garments you find in stores, even to improve upon them.

This book contains seventy of my favorite infantwear patterns. Preemie size also fits a 38cm (15") doll. Many of these patterns have been inspired by garments that have become favorites among those bought, received or made for my own children and for friends and relatives. Sometimes I see something I like in magazines and boutiques or on children passing by. I sketch what I like and make my own pattern and, at the same time, usually change and simplify the design. I have created many patterns especially for this book, choosing really simple, basic designs with as few details and pattern pieces as possible. Most are unisex so they can be worn by both baby boys and baby girls.

One of my favorite letters is from a mother who found my easy patterns a blessing after being frustrated by commercial patterns for children that "are so complicated and with so many pattern pieces that only somebody without children would have time to make them". I sincerely hope that you will find my patterns easy enough to encourage you to take the time to sew them.

All patterns were tested to be sure that they are easy enough to earn a place in this book. Simple, yet detailed line drawings allow you to see the potential value and versatility of each pattern. While sewing them, I was constantly thinking of shortcuts and taking notes in order to give you the simplest possible method.

Easy to enlarge and easy to sew, my patterns will save you lots of good money and help you in creating practical, comfortable and beautiful clothes for infants.

SIMPLE PATTERN ADJUSTMENTS

Compare the measurements of the child with the pattern, particularly sleeve length, garment length and width. If necessary, adjust the pattern size prior to cutting out the fabric. When convenient, make adjustments when enlarging the miniature pattern to full size. Use this simple method also to change pattern size to fit your child, if you are using designs from another age group.

To enlarge

Cut the pattern apart vertically and horizontally at several points. Spread the pieces apart until desired size is achieved. Slip a piece of paper underneath and tape it in place to bridge the separated pieces together. When enlarging a garment with sleeves, enlarge the sleeves as well to match the new, larger armhole. Draw the new outline.

To reduce

Pleat the pattern vertically and horizontally at several points until desired size is achieved. Tape the pleats in place. Or use pins so that you can easily remove them later, if you want to use the larger size when your child has grown into it.

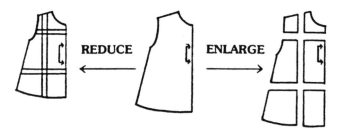

REDUCE ← → ENLARGE

PATTERN SIZES

This book contains patterns for infants in sizes from preemie to two-year-old.

Sizing was not easy because children's measurements differ so much. Therefore it's impossible to make patterns that would fit absolutely everybody in the same age group without any alterations.

I sized all patterns generously for average to taller-than-average infants of medium frame, with sufficient ease for proper fit and comfort. Generous lengths are designed into jackets, T-shirts and sleeves since infants grow so fast.

Handy tips are mentioned to extend the garment life for some of the patterns.

If your infant is much taller/shorter or chubbier/slimmer than mentioned below, enlarge/reduce pattern size prior to cutting out the fabric or, when convenient, when enlarging the pattern.

The patterns in this book are designed for the following five sizes:

Preemie size:	**up to 2 kg (4lb 4oz)**
	or up to 38 cm (15")
	also fits a 38cm (15") doll
0–3 months:	44–61 cm (17–24")
6 months:	up to 71 cm (28")
12 months:	up to 79 cm (31")
24 months:	up to 86 cm (34")

SEAM ALLOWANCES

Adult garments look good with narrow well-finished seam allowances. To avoid bulk, the seam allowances of infants' and children's clothes should also be narrow. The children grow mostly lengthwise and hardly at all in width, so I don't find it practical to use large seam allowances for growing-room except in length.

The patterns in my books INCLUDE the following seam and hem allowances (unless otherwise indicated):

Infants: 6mm (1/4") for seams, and 2½cm (1") for hem.
Children: 1cm (3/8") for seams and 2½-5cm (1-2") for hem.
Adults: 1cm (3/8") for seams and 2½cm (1") for hem. (Lengthen or shorten the pattern, if necessary, prior to cutting out the fabric.)

MARKS USED IN PATTERNS

———————— Cutting line.

  Place the pattern on fold of fabric. DO NOT CUT ON THIS LINE. (Fold always on lengthwise straight grain, except when on the bias, or otherwise indicated.)

— — — — — — — Gather. (Sew two rows of long stitches close to each other, and pull the bobbin threads to distribute fullness evenly into gathers.)

· · · · · · · · · · · · · · · · Folding line (or side line; or edge for pockets, facings, crotch).

 Place on straight lengthwise grain.

  Buttons, buttonholes.

1 2 3 4 Match same numbers when sewing.

PATTERNS AND INSTRUCTIONS

The first five designs in this book fit a preemie baby or a 38 cm (15") doll.

1. VEST (or minidress)
Size: Preemie or doll

Tiny undershirt, short sleeves and front closure. Self stretch binding around neck & sleeve ends. (Add a ruffle around lower edge for a minidress.)
Stretch fabrics only: Cotton knits, stretch terry, velour. **Fabric required:** 25x90cm (1/4ydx36"). **Notions:** Two tiny fasteners (or Velcro).

Sewing: Stitch shoulder seams. Press front edges under 2cm (3/4"). Bind raw edges of neck and sleeve ends with unifold stretch tape made of self fabric (see page 35). Stitch sleeves to armholes. Stitch sides and underarms. Sew on two tiny fasteners for front closure. Overlock lower edge.

2. FOOTED PULL-ON PANTS
Size: Preemie or doll

Very easy pattern without side seams. Elasticized waist.
Stretch fabrics only: Cotton knits, stretch terry, velour. **Fabric required:** 50x90cm (½ydx36"). **Notions:** Soft elastic for waist.

Sewing: Stitch center back and center front seams. To make pleats for heels, on wrong side of fabric pinch a 1.3cm (½") pleat across each back leg end (shown in pattern) and baste or pin it downward. Stitch seams around feet, inner legs and crotch. Sew waist edge down into a casing and insert soft elastic.

3. BONNET
Size: Preemie or doll

Soft and comfortable, double-layered for added warmth.
Stretch fabrics only: Cotton knits, stretch terry, velour. **Fabric required:** 30x90cm (1/3ydx36"). **Notions:** One tiny fastener (or Velcro).

Sewing: Stitch front and side sections to the back sections (both layers separately). Right sides in, stitch both layers together around all edges, leaving an opening at back. Clip curves, turn right side out, press and slipstitch opening closed. (If desired, topstitch close to entire outer edge.) Sew on one tiny fastener to close the flaps under the chin.

> Use a sheet of typing or tissue paper under any soft or sheer fabric, lace, or mesh, if you have trouble stitching it.

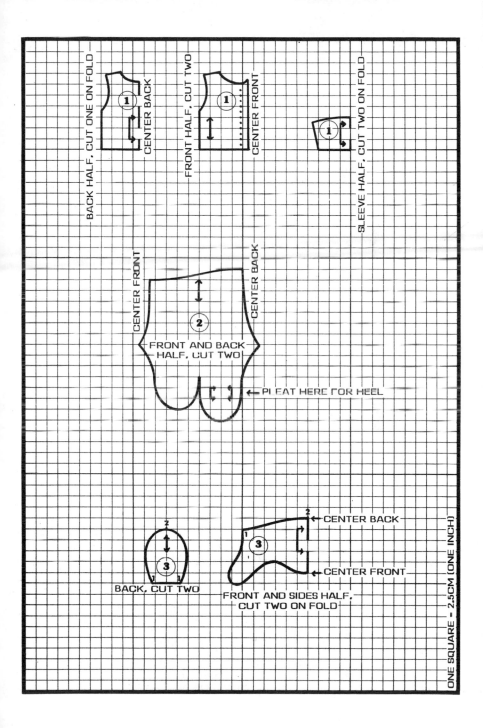

BACK HALF, CUT ONE ON FOLD

CENTER BACK

①

FRONT HALF, CUT TWO

CENTER FRONT

①

SLEEVE HALF, CUT TWO ON FOLD

①

CENTER FRONT

CENTER BACK

②

FRONT AND BACK HALF, CUT TWO

← PLEAT HERE FOR HEEL

2

③

BACK, CUT TWO

2
← CENTER BACK

③
1

← CENTER FRONT

FRONT AND SIDES HALF, CUT TWO ON FOLD

ONE SQUARE = 2.5CM (ONE INCH)

61

4. SLEEPER
Size: Preemie or doll

Raglan sleeves, fasteners on front and down one leg, self stretch binding around neck and sleeve ends, no side seams, easy pleats for heels.
Stretch fabrics only: Cotton knits, stretch terry, velour. (Flame-retardant fabrics are required by law on children's sleepwear.) **Fabric required:** 50x90cm (½ydx36"). **Notions:** Velcro (or snap fastener tape).

Sewing: Trim 2cm (3/4") off the <u>right</u> leg seam allowances (shown with dots in the pattern). Stitch center back seam. Bind sleeve ends with unifold stretch tape made of self fabric (page 35). Stitch underarms of sleeves. Stitch sleeves to armhole edges of front and back. Make pleats for heels (see pattern #2). Stitch seam around right foot and inner leg to crotch. Stitch seam around left foot up to seam allowance for the fastener tape. Bind neck edge with unifold stretch tape. Sew fastener tape to center front and left leg opening.

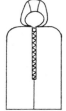

5. BUNTING BAG
Size: Preemie or doll

Lined or unlined, this hooded bunting bag with front zipper keeps your tiny bundle toasty warm and cozy.
Suggested fabrics: Soft warm fabrics such as corduroy, quilted fabrics, wool duffle or old lightweight blanket. Or use windproof and water resistant fabrics such as poplin, nylon-coated fabrics or fake fur. If you use thin or slippery fabrics, line the bag with flannelette. **Fabric required:** 55x90cm (22x36") for the bag, the same amount for optional lining. **Notions:** 25cm (10") long zipper, foldover braid (or doublefold bias tape) for binding front edges and hood edge.

Sewing: Stitch hood center panel between the sides. Stitch curved shoulder seams. Stitch hood to neck edge. Bind front edges and hood edges with foldover braid (or doublefold bias tape). Stitch zipper in place. Stitch center front seam below zipper. Center front matching center back, stitch bottom seam closed. (If desired, embroider the bag by hand or machine or decorate it with appliqués prior to sewing the seams. The hood or the entire bag can be made double-layered or lined for added warmth. If desired, stitch a casing made from a fabric strip to the wrong side of hood front edge and insert a cord.)

Important: Tiny babies like to sleep with arms folded across the chest. They are comfortable and warm in that position. Since this bunting bag is designed without sleeves, make sure your baby will not slide to the bottom <u>by not using</u> slippery fabrics <u>or by lining</u> the entire bag with soft, tightly-woven flannelette. If too long, fold excess length under, or temporarily topstitch across the bottom to make it shorter until full length is needed.

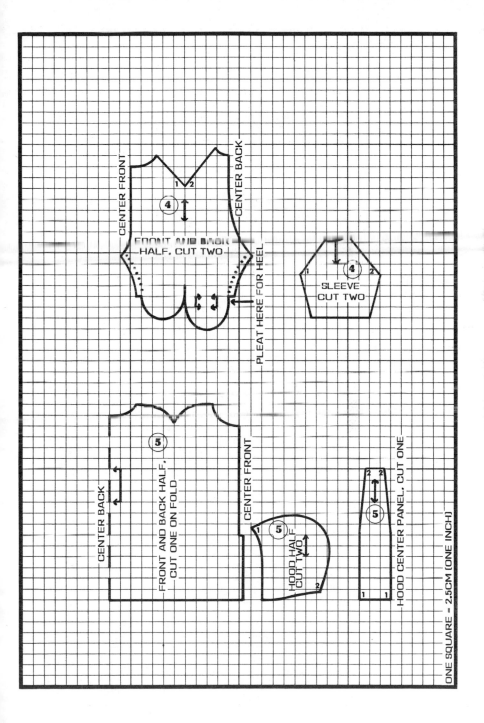

CENTER FRONT

CENTER BACK

FRONT AND BACK
HALF, CUT TWO

④

PLEAT HERE FOR HEEL

SLEEVE
CUT TWO

1 ④ 2

CENTER BACK

⑤

FRONT AND BACK HALF,
CUT ONE ON FOLD

CENTER FRONT

HOOD HALF
CUT TWO

⑤

HOOD CENTER PANEL, CUT ONE

⑤

ONE SQUARE = 2.5CM (ONE INCH)

63

6. DRAWSTRING NIGHTGOWN
Size: 0-3 months

Envelope neck with self stretch binding, drawstring for tucking feet in, elasticized wrists. (When too short, remove the cord from lower edge casing, cut elasticized sleeve ends off and hem sleeve ends narrowly.)
Stretch fabrics only: Cotton knits, stretch terry, cotton velour. (Flame-retardant fabrics are required by law on children's sleepwear.) **Fabric required:** 70x90cm (3/4ydx36"). **Notions:** Narrow elastic, 140cm (55") long ribbon.

Sewing: Bind raw neck and shoulder edges of front and back with unifold stretch tape made of self fabric (see page 35). Lap back shoulder extensions over front ones, matching shoulder lines, pin or baste in place. Stitch sleeves to armholes. Stitch sides and underarms. Sew sleeve ends under into casings and insert soft elastic. Sew lower edge under into a casing and insert a ribbon.

7. JUMPSUIT OR ROMPER
Size: 0-3 months

Loose-fitting design, front and back gathered to rib knit chestband, rib knit legbands, shoulder straps or tie-ons. Or make romper with elasticized leg ends. (When jumpsuit becomes too short, convert it into pull-on pants or romper.)
Suggested fabrics: Soft cotton types, pinwale corduroy, eyelet, flannelette, cotton knits, velour, fleece. **Fabric required:** 50x90cm (½ydx36"). **Notions:** Rib knit.

Sewing jumpsuit: Sew shoulder straps (or tie-ons if preferred). Pin strap ends between upper edges of the two chestband layers, right sides in and all raw edges even, and stitch the bands together along upper edge from end to end. Be sure to use stretch stitch. Open out the band and, right sides together, stitch band ends together at center back. Turn the band right side out and press in half. Stitch center back and center front seams. Gather upper edge and stitch it to chestband. Stitch inner leg seams. Stitch rib knit bands to leg ends. (**Romper:** Elasticize leg ends.)

Doublefold bias tape makes quick drawstring ties; edgestitch the tape closed from right side through all thicknesses.

With fusible web, iron soft fleece between the two layers of fabric that you wish to quilt.

Clean your old spiral mascara brush with cleaning lotion or oil, then thoroughly wash with soap and water. The brush is great for removing lint and fuzz under throat plate and around bobbin.

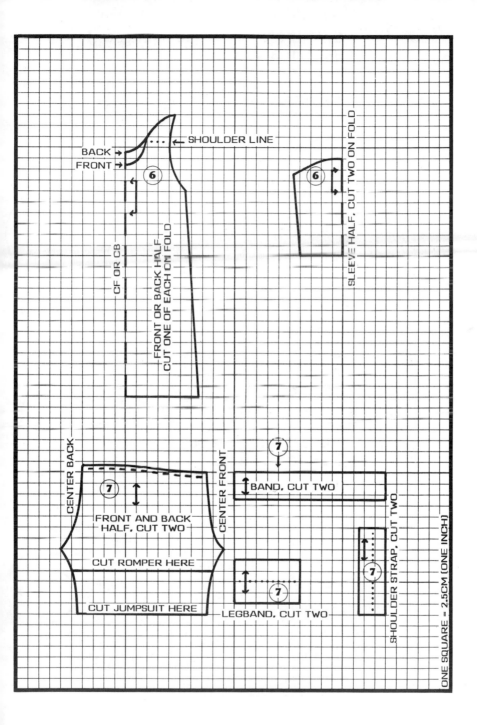

SHOULDER LINE

BACK →
FRONT →

(6)

CF OR CB

FRONT OR BACK HALF
CUT ONE OF EACH ON FOLD

SLEEVE HALF, CUT TWO ON FOLD

(6)

CENTER BACK

(7)

FRONT AND BACK
HALF, CUT TWO

CUT ROMPER HERE

CUT JUMPSUIT HERE

CENTER FRONT

(7)

BAND, CUT TWO

LEGBAND, CUT TWO

(7)

SHOULDER STRAP, CUT TWO

(7)

ONE SQUARE = 2.5CM (ONE INCH)

65

8. T-SHIRT (or dress, nightgown)
Size: 0-3 months

Envelope neck with self stretch binding, short sleeves. (Lengthen for nightie, add a ruffle for minidress.)
Stretch fabrics only: Cotton knits, stretch terry, velour.
Fabric required: 50x90cm (½ydx36") makes two.

Sewing: Bind raw neck edges of front and back with unifold stretch tape (see page 35). Lap back shoulder extensions over front ones, matching shoulder lines, pin or baste. Overlock sleeve ends, press them under and topstitch in place. Stitch sleeves to armholes. Stitch sides and underarms. Overlock lower edge and topstitch it under.

9. PLAYSUIT OR SLEEPER
Size: 0-3 months

Easy pleats for heels, button/buttonhole closure, self stretch binding. Make a shirt (#8) to wear under this playsuit for cool days. (When too short, make playsuit into pull-on pants, cut feet off and add rib knit legbands.)
Stretch fabrics only: Cotton knits, stretch terry, velour. (Flame-retardant fabrics are required by law on children's sleepwear.) **Fabric required:** 60x90cm (2/3ydx36"). **Notions:** Two buttons.

Sewing: Sew an appliqué onto front or back if desired. Stitch back half of the crotch piece between legs of back section. Make pleats for heels (see #2). Stitch sides, around leg ends and inner leg seams, connecting the front half of the crotch at the same time. Bind raw edges of underarms-shoulders-neck with unifold stretch tape (see page 35). Add buttons/buttonholes to flap ends.

10. JUMPER OR SUNDRESS
Size: 0-3 months

Single- or double-layered design wraps across back, straps buttoned to front bib. If desired, make it reversible by using two different fabrics for double-layered version.
Suggested fabrics: Lightweight cotton types, pinwale corduroy, eyelet, broadcloth, calico. **Fabric required:** 60x90cm (2/3ydx36"), twice for double-layered version. **Notions:** Two (or four) buttons. Doublefold bias tape or lace for binding edges of single-layered version.

Sewing double-layered: Right sides in, stitch both layers together around all edges, leaving an opening. Trim corners and clip curves, turn right side out, slipstitch opening closed, press. Make buttonholes to bib front and sew on buttons at both sides of each strap end. If desired, sew an appliqué onto front prior to stitching the two layers together. **Single-layered:** Bind all raw edges with doublefold bias tape or folded lace. Add buttons and buttonholes.

Press as you sew.

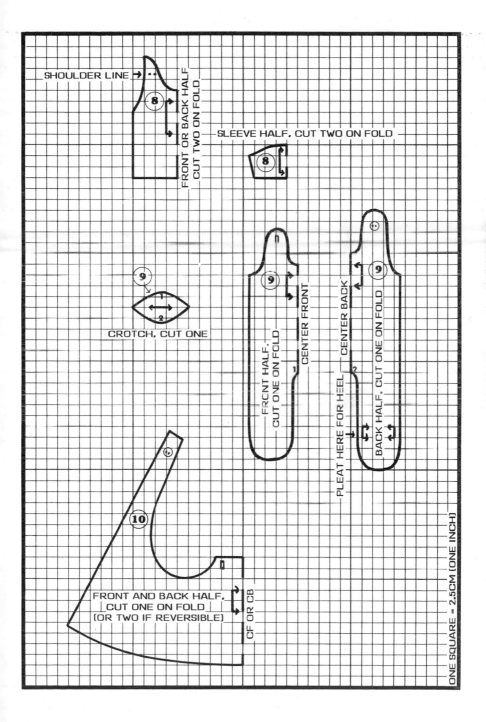

SHOULDER LINE →

FRONT OR BACK HALF, CUT TWO ON FOLD

SLEEVE HALF, CUT TWO ON FOLD

CROTCH, CUT ONE

FRONT HALF, CUT ONE ON FOLD

CENTER FRONT

PLEAT HERE FOR HEEL

CENTER BACK

BACK HALF, CUT ONE ON FOLD

FRONT AND BACK HALF, CUT ONE ON FOLD (OR TWO IF REVERSIBLE)

CF OR CB

ONE SQUARE = 2.5CM (ONE INCH)

11. VEST (or top or dress)
Size: 0-3 months

Cross-over vest or top with raglan sleeves. Self stretch binding. (Add a ruffle for minidress.)
Stretch fabrics only: Cotton knits, stretch terry, velour.
Fabric required: 50x90cm (½ydx36").

Sewing: Stitch sleeves to armhole edges of front and back. Bind raw edges of sleeve ends and entire neck opening with unifold stretch tape (see page 35). Overlap fronts, stitch side and underarm seams. Bind lower edge with unifold stretch tape.

12. PANTIES
Size: 0-3 months

Neat and comfortable, covering all the tummy and reaching up to underarms. Elasticized waist.
Stretch fabrics only: Cotton knits, stretch terry, velour.
Fabric required: 60x90cm (2/3ydx36"), makes two panties.
Notions: Elastic for waist.

Sewing: Overlock outer edges of leg facings. Stitch facings to legholes. Open facings out, stitch side seams and facing ends. Turn facings to inside and topstitch them in place. Sew casing in waist edge, insert elastic.

13. BABY BONNET
Size: 0-3 months

Ties under chin. Self stretch binding.
Stretch fabrics only: Cotton knits, stretch terry, velour.
Fabric required: 30x90cm (1/3ydx36"). **Notions:** Two 25cm (10") long ribbons.

Sewing: Stitch center panel between side sections. Bind all raw edges with bifold stretch tape (see page 35). Attach ribbons.

14. BABY BOOTIES
Size: 0-3 months

Easy and comfortable booties to keep tiny toes warm, elasticized ankles keep booties in place.
Stretch fabrics only: Cotton knits, stretch terry, velour.
Fabric required: 25x90cm (1/4ydx36"). **Notions:** Elastic.

Sewing: Overlock raw upper edge of each bootie. Turn facing allowance of each ankle under, stitch close to raw edge. Stitch again 1.3cm (½") from the first stitching line, forming a casing. Insert narrow elastic (12cm or 4 3/4" long) through casing, stitch ends securely to casing ends. Stitch front seam. Pin or baste lower edge all around the sole (wider part at front), stitch.

> The more you sew, the better you get and the easier it will be.

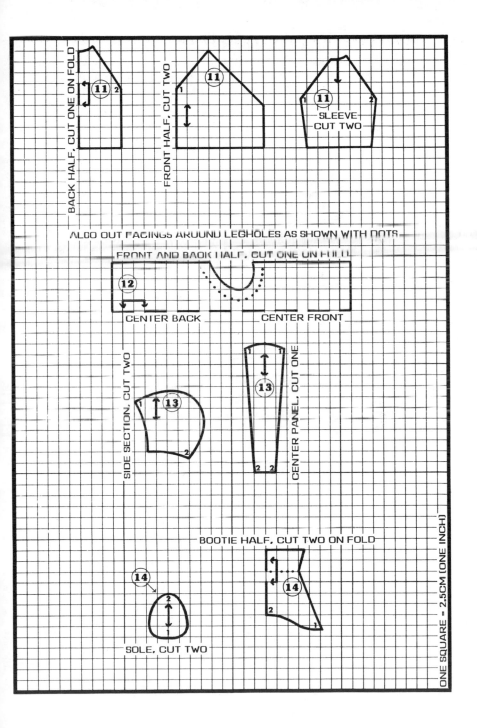

BACK HALF, CUT ONE ON FOLD

(11) 2

FRONT HALF, CUT TWO

1 (11)

(11)

SLEEVE
CUT TWO

ALSO CUT FACINGS AROUND LEGHOLES AS SHOWN WITH DOTS

FRONT AND BACK HALF, CUT ONE ON FOLD

(12)

CENTER BACK   CENTER FRONT

SIDE SECTION, CUT TWO

(13)

CENTER PANEL, CUT ONE

(13)

BOOTIE HALF, CUT TWO ON FOLD

(14)

(14)

SOLE, CUT TWO

ONE SQUARE = 2.5CM (ONE INCH)

69

15. OUTDOOR SUIT
Size: 0-3 months

Warm and cozy hooded suit, raglan sleeves with closed sleeve ends, leg ends closed with soles, front zipper. Big enough to wear over other clothing. (When too short, open sleeve ends and remove soles, stitch rib knit bands to sleeve and leg ends.)

Suggested fabrics: Soft and warm fabrics such as wool duffle, thick knits, fake fur, quilted fabrics, thick corduroy. Windproof, water resistant fabrics such as poplin and nylon-coated fabrics lined with soft flannelette. **Fabric required:** 1mx115cm (1ydx45"), plus optional lining. **Notions:** Foldover braid for hood front edge and front opening (or make your own doublefold bias tape from any suitable fabric), 25cm (10") long zipper.

Sewing: Stitch underarms and around sleeve ends. Stitch sleeves to armhole edges of front and back. Stitch center back seam. Stitch center front seam from crotch up to where the zipper will end. Stitch inner leg seams. Stitch soles to leg ends. Stitch hood back seam. Stitch hood to neck opening. Bind raw edges of hood front and zipper opening with foldover braid or doublefold bias tape. Sew zipper in place. (If desired, sew a strip of fake fur to hood's front edge.)

16. SLEEPER OR PLAYSUIT
Size: 0-3 months

Sleeve tops and upper edges of front and back gathered to double-layered rib knit yoke, snap closure at inner leg seams, easy pleats for heels.

Suggested fabrics: Sleeves and bodice - Cotton knits, stretch terry, velour, fleece, pinwale corduroy, cotton and blends, eyelet. Yoke and sleevebands - Rib knit. (Flame-retardant fabrics are required by law on children's sleepwear.) **Fabric required:** Bodice and sleeves - 70x90cm (3/4ydx36"). **Notions:** Rib knit for yoke and sleevebands: 15x45cm (6x17"). Snap fastener tape (or Velcro) for inner legs.

Sewing: Stitch center back and center front seams. Right sides of yokes together, stitch shoulder seams for 2½cm (1") in from outside edges toward neck (shown with dots in the pattern), lock the stitching securely at neck edge. Turn right sides out so you have the neck opening in the middle, press. Gather upper edges of front and back and stitch them to yoke. Stitch underarms of sleeves. Gather sleeve tops and stitch the sleeves to armholes. Stitch rib knit bands to sleeve ends. Pleat the heels (see #2). Stitch around leg ends to where seam allowances for inner leg openings begin. Sew snap fastener tape to inner leg seam allowances.

Neat tip: If snaps are constantly opening, flatten the balls slightly by tapping them gently with a hammer over a hard surface.

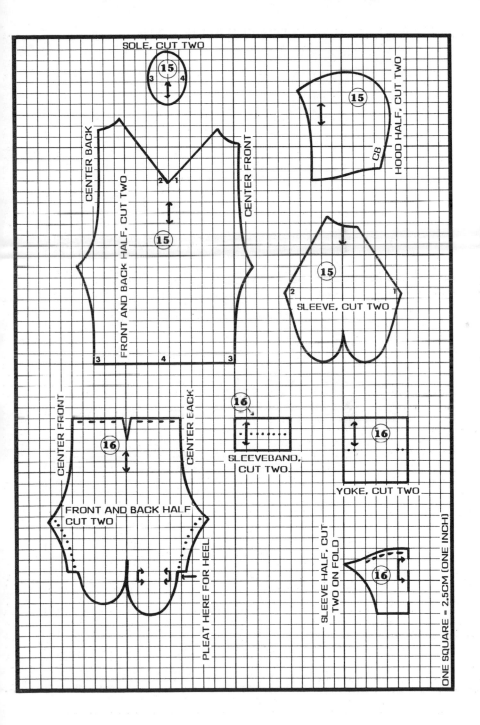

SOLE, CUT TWO

15
3   4

HOOD HALF, CUT TWO

15

CB

CENTER BACK

FRONT AND BACK HALF, CUT TWO

2 1

15

CENTER FRONT

15

2   1

SLEEVE, CUT TWO

CENTER FRONT

16

FRONT AND BACK HALF
CUT TWO

CENTER BACK

PLEAT HERE FOR HEEL

16

SLEEVEBAND,
CUT TWO

16

YOKE, CUT TWO

SLEEVE HALF, CUT
TWO ON FOLD

16

ONE SQUARE = 2.5CM (ONE INCH)

71

17. BUNTING BAG
Size: 0-3 months

Suggested fabrics are the same as for design #5. **Fabric required:** 1mx115cm (1ydx45"). **Notions:** 35cm (14") long zipper, foldover braid or doublefold bias tape.

Sewing: See design #5.

Need fabric strips for bias or stretchy tapes? Cut the strip first from self-adhesive vinyl, peel off the paper, stick vinyl onto fabric, and cut along the edges. Pull vinyl off and reuse it. No marking, folding or pins. Fabric won't slide or stretch.

Cut basic patterns from interfacing to use them repeatedly. Some stores even sell interfacing printed with one inch grid (or with dots spaced an inch apart).

Have your children make large envelopes for your patterns out of their school papers and drawings. A great way to save both!

Make children's summer pyjamas out of fabric remnants. Cut each pattern piece in a different color for a wild look that kids love.

Before applying zipper, stabilize stretch fabric edge with seam binding or fusible interfacing.

Even oil gets old. If you bought your sewing machine oil years ago, it's time to buy a new bottle.

Before you sew the garment, use a scrap fabric to check stitch length and the successful combination of needle and thread size.

Instead of basting, use masking tape to keep zipper in place; stitch along tape's side, not through it.

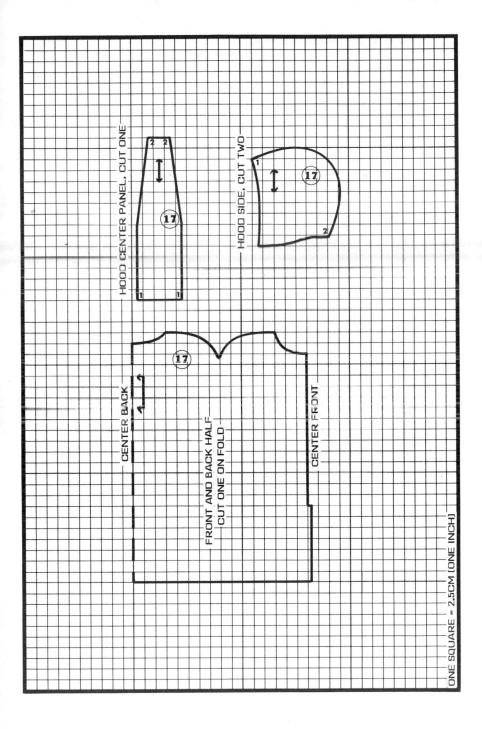

HOOD CENTER PANEL, CUT ONE

HOOD SIDE, CUT TWO

17

17

CENTER BACK

FRONT AND BACK HALF
CUT ONE ON FOLD

CENTER FRONT

17

ONE SQUARE = 2.5CM (ONE INCH)

18. SLEEPER
Size: 6 months

Raglan sleeves, no side seams, front zipper continues down one leg, easy pleats for heels, elastic across midback. (When too short, make it into pull-on pants with elasticized waist, cut feet off and add rib knit legbands.)
Stretch fabrics only: Cotton knits, stretch terry, velour. (Flame-retardant fabrics are required by law on children's sleepwear.) **Fabric required:** 1mx115cm (1ydx45") including enough fabric for sleevebands and neckband. **Notions:** 45cm (18") long zipper, one fastener for neckband. (Rib knit for sleevebands and neckband if not made of self fabric.)

<u>Sewing:</u> Sew an appliqué onto front or sleeves if desired. Stitch center back seam. Stitch underarms. Stitch sleeves to armhole edges of front and back. Trim 2cm (3/4") off <u>left</u> inner leg seam allowances (shown with dots in the pattern). To make pleats for heels, on wrong side of fabric pinch a 2cm (3/4") pleat across each back leg end (shown in pattern) and baste or pin it downward. Stitch seam around left foot and inner leg to crotch. Stitch seam around right foot up to seam allowance for the zipper. Sew zipper to front opening. Stitch bands to sleeve ends. Stitch band around neck so that the right side of band end will extend and lap over the left one (to protect baby's neck from zipper). Sew on a fastener for neckband closure.

19. BALACLAVA HELMET
Sizes: 6 months and 24 months

Very comfortable, no ribbons or buttons, rib knit band around face opening. Protects ears, neck and forehead. Excellent also under hoods. Two sizes are shown in the pattern.
Stretch fabrics only: Cotton knits, stretch terry, velour. **Fabric required:** 35x90cm (14x36"). **Notions:** Rib knit.

<u>Sewing:</u> Stitch center back and center front seams. Overlock lower edge. Stitch rib knit band around face opening.

For an easy-to-move seam guide, slip a rubber band around your sewing machine's freearm.

Save the elastic waistbands from worn pantyhose and use them for children's clothes.

Affix an appliqué or a patch securely in place with a strip of fusible web so you can stitch around it without pins.

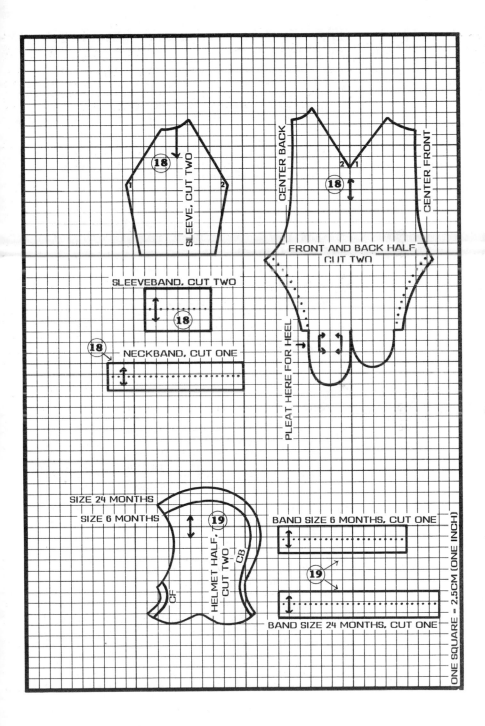

SLEEVE, CUT TWO
18
1 2

CENTER BACK

18
2 1

CENTER FRONT

FRONT AND BACK HALF
CUT TWO

PLEAT HERE FOR HEEL

SLEEVEBAND, CUT TWO
18

NECKBAND, CUT ONE
18

SIZE 24 MONTHS
SIZE 6 MONTHS
19
HELMET HALF, CUT TWO
CB
CF

BAND SIZE 6 MONTHS, CUT ONE
19
BAND SIZE 24 MONTHS, CUT ONE

ONE SQUARE = 2.5CM (ONE INCH)

20. TANK TOP (or dress, nightgown)
Size: 6 months

Simple design with self stretch binding. (Lenghten the pattern for nightgown. Add a ruffle around lower edge for minidress.)
Stretch fabrics only: Cotton knits, stretch terry, rib knit, velour. **Fabric required:** 35x90cm (14x36"), makes two tops.

Sewing: Stitch left shoulder seam. Bind raw neck edge with unifold stretch tape made of self fabric (see page 35). Stitch right shoulder seam. Bind armhole edges with stretch tape. Stitch side seams. Overlock lower edge, press it under and topstitch in place.

21. DRESS OR CHRISTENING GOWN
Size: 6 months

Dress: Loose-fitting design, upper edge gathered to rib knit neckband. Short or long puffed sleeves with rib knit bands.
Suggested fabrics: Cotton and blends, calico, broadcloth, pinwale corduroy, eyelet, cotton knits, velour, fleece. **Fabric required:** 70x90cm (3/4dx36"). **Notions:** Rib knit.

Sewing dress: Stitch shoulder seams. Gather sleeve tops and stitch sleeves to armholes. Stitch sides and underarms. Gather neck opening and stitch neckband to it. Gather sleeve ends and stitch rib knit bands to them. Overlock lower edge, press it under and topstitch in place.

Long christening gown: This design can easily be converted into a charming christening gown. Side seam length of finished gown is about 1 metre (39½"). Make a bonnet with pattern #13 and trim it with ruffled lace ribbons.
Suggested fabrics: Fine cotton, lace, eyelet, silk types, satin. **Fabric required:** 150x115cm (1 2/3 yd x 45"). **Notions:** 4.50 metres (5 yards) of about 5cm (2") wide lace or eyelet, three small buttons, doublefold bias tape.

Sewing christening gown: Lengthen the pattern so that the side seams become 70cm (27½") long. Cut center front on fold. Cut long sleeves. Cut two back sections with back edges on fabric selvages and add 2cm (3/4") facing allowances to back edges for button closure. Stitch shoulder seams. Trim sleeve ends with lace. On inside, stitch stretched elastic around wrists 5cm (2") from sleeve ends, forming self ruffles. Gather or pleat sleeve tops and stitch the sleeves to armholes. Stitch sides and underarms. Stitch lace around lower edge. Gather or pleat a ruffle (20x230cm or 8x90") and stitch it around the hem to lower edge of lace. Stitch lace around ruffle lower edge. Press facing allowances of center back under and topstitch them in place. Stitch lace around neck opening, gather raw neck edge (fabric and lace together) and bind it with bias tape. Make buttonholes and sew on buttons for back closure from neck to waist.

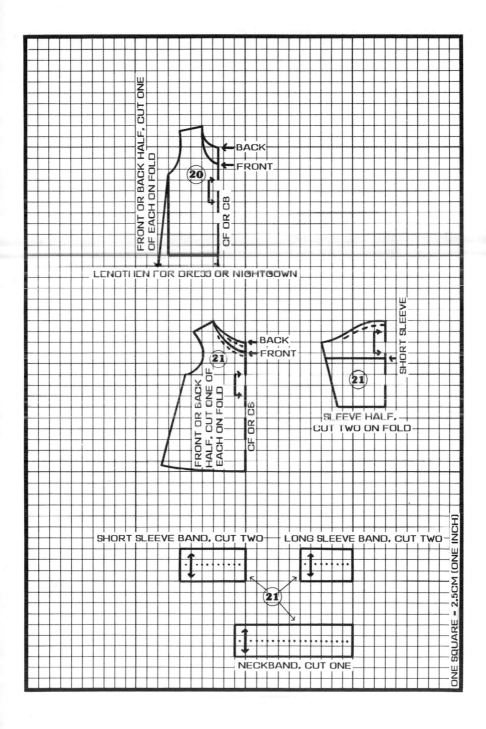

FRONT OR BACK HALF, CUT ONE OF EACH ON FOLD

BACK
FRONT

20

CF OR CB

LENGTHEN FOR DRESS OR NIGHTGOWN

BACK
FRONT

21

FRONT OR BACK HALF, CUT ONE OF EACH ON FOLD

CF OR CB

SHORT SLEEVE

21

SLEEVE HALF, CUT TWO ON FOLD

SHORT SLEEVE BAND, CUT TWO

LONG SLEEVE BAND, CUT TWO

21

NECKBAND, CUT ONE

ONE SQUARE = 2.5CM (ONE INCH)

77

22. ROMPER
Size: 6 months

Self stretch binding. Elasticized legholes. Button closure at crotch.
Stretch fabrics only: Cotton knits, stretch terry, velour, rib knit. **Fabric required:** 50x90cm (½ydx36"). **Notions:** Two buttons.

Sewing: Gather upper edges until 15cm (6") long each. Cut two fabric strips 4x15cm (1½x6") each, press into trifold tapes (see page 35) and stitch to upper edges. Cut two fabric strips 4x25cm (1½x10") each, press into trifold tapes and edgestitch them in place (middle of tape forms a shoulder strap with ends binding underarms). Stitch side seams. On inside, zigzag gently stretched elastic to leghole edges. Bind elasticized edges and crotch flaps with trifold stretch tape. Make buttonholes and sew on buttons for crotch closure.

23. PLAYSUIT
Size: 6 months

Short sleeves, self stretch binding around neck, button closures at right shoulder and crotch, elasticized legholes.
Stretch fabrics only: Cotton knits, stretch terry, velour. **Fabric required:** 50x90cm (½ydx36"). **Notions:** Narrow elastic, four buttons.

Sewing: Trim 2.5cm (1") off left shoulder seam allowances. Stitch left shoulder seam. Bind neck edge with unifold stretch tape (see page 35). Press under 2.5cm (1") on both front and back right shoulder edges, topstitch closed. Lap front shoulder over back one 1.2cm (½"), pin or baste. Stitch sleeves to armholes. Bind raw sleeve ends with unifold stretch tape. Stitch sides and underarms. On inside, zigzag gently stretched elastic to leghole edges, turn elasticized edges under and edgestitch in place. Turn facing allowances of crotch under, lap front over back. Make buttonholes and sew on buttons for crotch and shoulder closure.

24. DRESS
Size: 6 months

Skirt gathered to yoke, lace trim, self stretch binding around neck, a slit with button at back.
Suggested fabrics: Cotton knits, cotton and blends, eyelet, seersucker. **Fabric required:** 50x90cm (½ydx36"). **Notions:** Lace, one button.

Sewing: Slit center back 5cm (2") from neck down. Stitch shoulder seams. Bind neck opening and the slit edges with doublefold bias tape made of self fabric (see page 34-35). Gather upper edges of skirt front and back and stitch them to yoke. Trim armholes and lower edge with lace. Stitch side seams. Sew on a small button and loop for back closure.

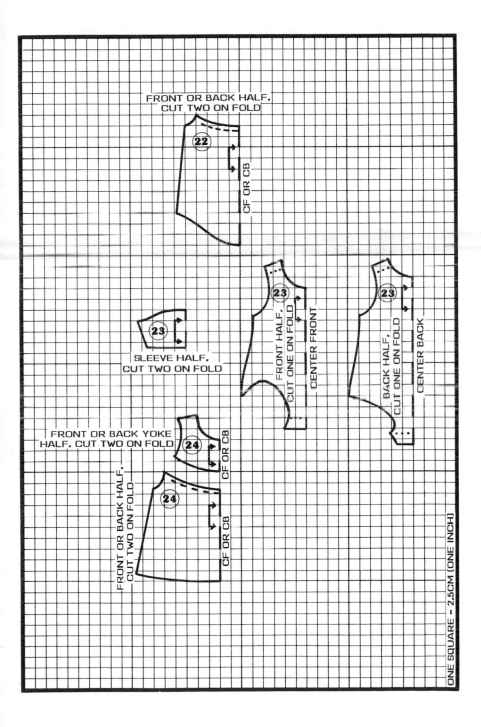

FRONT OR BACK HALF,
CUT TWO ON FOLD

22

CF OR CB

23

SLEEVE HALF,
CUT TWO ON FOLD

23

FRONT HALF,
CUT ONE ON FOLD

CENTER FRONT

23

BACK HALF,
CUT ONE ON FOLD

CENTER BACK

FRONT OR BACK YOKE
HALF, CUT TWO ON FOLD

24

CF OR CB

24

FRONT OR BACK HALF,
CUT TWO ON FOLD

CF OR CB

ONE SQUARE = 2.5CM (ONE INCH)

25. BUNTING BAG (COVERALLS)
Size: 6 months (Coveralls: 12 months)

Drawstring hood, closed-end raglan sleeves, full-length separating zipper at front and down one leg. Edges of hood front and zipper opening trimmed with bias binding or foldover braid. (When too short, you can convert it into coveralls. Rib knit bands around sleeve ends and leg ends. Elasticized back waist.)

Suggested fabrics: Make it of soft and warm, lightweight fabric such as wool duffle, quilted fabrics, thick corduroy. Or use windproof and water resistant fabrics such as poplin or nylon-coated fabrics lined with soft flannelette. **Fabric required:** 120x140cm (1 1/4 yd x 55"), the same additional amount for optional lining. **Notions:** 75cm (30") long separating zipper, cord for hood drawstring, a strip (4x46cm or 1½x18") of any suitable fabric for hood casing, doublefold bias tape or foldover braid. Additionally needed when converting the bag into coveralls: Rib knit 15x71cm (6x28"), elastic for waist. (Save fabric scrap for crotch piece.)

Sewing bunting bag: Stitch center back seam. Stitch underarms and sleeve ends closed. Stitch sleeves to armhole edges of front and back. Cut right side only, from waist all the way down, as shown with dots in the pattern, for zipper opening. Stitch center front seam, from bottom up, to the cut section. Stitch hood center panel between side sections. To prepare the strip for hood casing, stitch raw ends under, press one long edge under and stitch the strip to hood's front edge on the wrong side of fabric, raw strip edge along raw hood edge, sewing close to both edges and leaving ends open. Stitch hood to neck opening. Bind hood front edge and both edges of zipper opening with bias tape or foldover braid. Sew zipper in place to front opening from hood edge all the way down to bottom (there will be about 5cm or 2" excess length of zipper at bottom which will be needed when converting the bag into coveralls). Right sides together, center front matching center back and with zipper excess extending, stitch bottom closed ("jump" stitching over zipper coils). Insert cord through hood casing. (See safety tip mentioned for bunting bag #5.)

Converting bunting bag into coveralls: Open sleeve ends and bottom. From bottom upward, rip open 30½cm (12") in both center front and center back seams. Stitch inner leg seams, attaching additional crotch piece (shown in the pattern) between the legs at the same time. Stitch rib knit bands to sleeve ends and left leg end. Right leg end: Fold rib knit band in half lengthwise, stitch each end closed, turn right side out, and stitch the band around leg end. Sew zipper's lower end, previously left unsewn, to each end of rib knit legband. On inside, stitch stretched elastic across back waist.

Reduce lint by turning garments inside out for laundering.

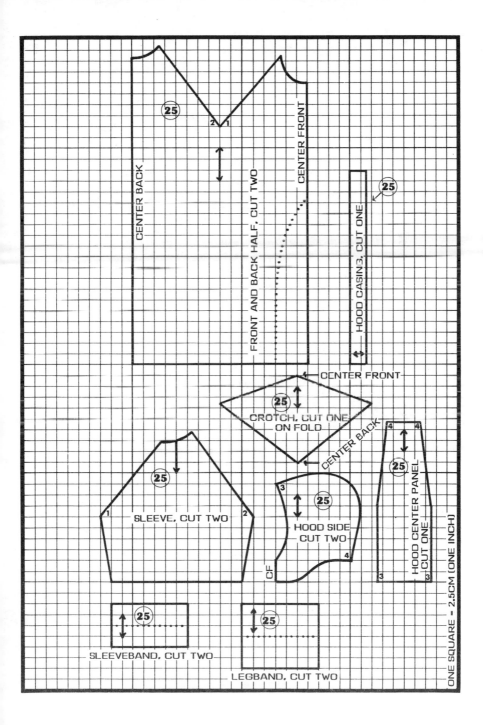

81

26. TWO BIBS
Size: 6 months

Simple bib with pocket and ties. Second bib has Velcro-fastened flaps.

Suggested fabrics: Vinyl or vinyl-coated fabric, terry cloth, quilted fabrics. **Fabric required:** 50x90cm (½ydx36"), makes two bibs. **Notions:** About 2 metres (2 yards) of doublefold bias tape for each design. Velcro for second bib.

Sewing tie-on bib: Sew an appliqué onto pocket if desired. Bind upper edge of pocket with bias tape. Baste or pin the pocket in place. Bind all edges, except the neck, with bias tape. Bind the neck edge with the remaining piece of bias tape, leaving the ends extending at each side for ties and edgestitching from end to end. If you find it difficult to catch both layers with straight stitch, use wide zigzag instead.

Sewing Velcro-attached bib: Sew as above but bind all edges, including the neck edge, with bias tape. Sew a piece of Velcro to flap ends.

Neat tip: Keep the pocket open by stuffing a paper towel in it to catch crumbs and absorb spills.

27. COVER-UP BIB
Size: 6 months

This loose-fitting design with large pocket and long sleeves with elasticized wrists covers all front, shoulders and also arms. It is easy to enlarge for an older child as a handy cover-up for nursery school to protect clothing at mealtimes and for crafts.

Suggested fabrics: Vinyl or vinyl-coated fabrics, nylon, terry cloth, smooth and tightly-woven polyester. **Fabric required:** 50x90cm (½ydx36"). **Notions:** Elastic for wrists, about 2½ metres (2 2/3 yards) of doublefold bias tape.

Sewing: Sew an appliqué onto pocket or front if desired. Bind upper edge of pocket with bias tape. On inside, stitch stretched elastic to sleeve ends, turn elasticized edges under and edgestitch them in place. Pin or baste pocket in place. Stitch underarms. Beginning at inside corner of one shoulder, bind raw edges of shoulders, sides and bottom with bias tape. Take the remaining piece of bias tape (about 76cm or 30" long) and stitch it around the neck, edgestitching from end to end, with ends extending at each side for ties.

Permanently glue an extra measuring tape to the edge of your sewing table. Practical!

When using stiff fabrics for ruffles, cut them on the bias or in a circular shape.

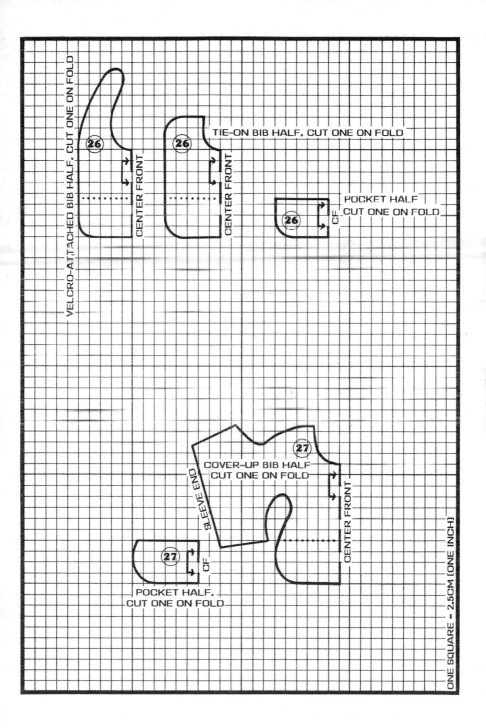

VELCRO-ATTACHED BIB HALF, CUT ONE ON FOLD

(26)

CENTER FRONT

TIE-ON BIB HALF, CUT ONE ON FOLD

(26)

CENTER FRONT

POCKET HALF
CUT ONE ON FOLD

(26)

CF

COVER-UP BIB HALF
CUT ONE ON FOLD

(27)

SLEEVE END

CENTER FRONT

POCKET HALF,
CUT ONE ON FOLD

(27)

CF

ONE SQUARE = 2.5CM (ONE INCH)

28. HOODED JACKET
Size: 6 months

Raglan sleeves and drawstring hood, rib knit bands around sleeve ends and waist. Kangaroo pockets. Buttons and buttonholes or snap fasteners for front closure.
Stretch fabrics only: Velour, stretch terry, mediumweight cotton knits, synthetic knits. Also fleece. **Fabric required:** 60x90cm (2/3ydx45"). **Notions:** Rib knit, cord for hood drawstring, five buttons or snap fastener tape.

Sewing: Overlock bias edge of each pocket, topstitch them under, press upper edge and longer side of each pocket under and topstitch pockets in place. Stitch sleeves to armhole edges of front and back. Stitch side seams (catching pocket sides between the seam) and underarms. Stitch hood back seam. Overlock hood front edge, press under 2.5cm (1"), edgestitch in place forming a casing (turn ends of casing allowance under on the bias). Press front facing allowances under 2½cm (1"). Turn front facings to outside. Stitch hood to neck edge, at the same time stitching upper facing ends closed (the front edges will extend 2½cm or 1" beyond hood edges). Stitch rib knit bands to sleeve ends. Stitch each waistband end closed, turn right side out and press the entire band in half. Stitch the band around waist with front ends of band sandwiched between facing allowance and garment. Make buttonholes and sew on buttons (or snap fastener tape) for front closure. Insert a cord for hood drawstring.

29. JUMPSUIT
Size: 6 months

Loose-fitting pants without side seams gathered to rib knit yoke. Button closure on shoulders and at waistline side slits. Snap fastener tape along inner leg seams. Rib knit legbands.
Suggested fabrics: Corduroy, velour, cotton knits, fleece. **Fabric required:** 50x90cm (½ydx36"). **Notions:** Rib knit 20x90cm (8x36"), six buttons, snap fastener tape for inner leg seams, doublefold bias tape.

Sewing: Slit sides 5cm (2") from waist down (as shown in the pattern). Bind slit edges with bias tape. Stitch center back and center front seams. To prepare yoke, stitch two front sections together at sides, armholes, shoulders and neck, trim corners and clip curves, turn right side out and press. Prepare back sections the same way. Gather upper edge of pants front and back and stitch to yoke. Make buttonholes and sew on buttons for closure at shoulders and side slits (lap front over back). Press under 1.3cm (½") of inner leg seam allowances. Sew each end of both legbands closed, turn right side out and press. Sew these prepared rib knit bands to leg ends. Sew snap fastener tape to inner leg seams.

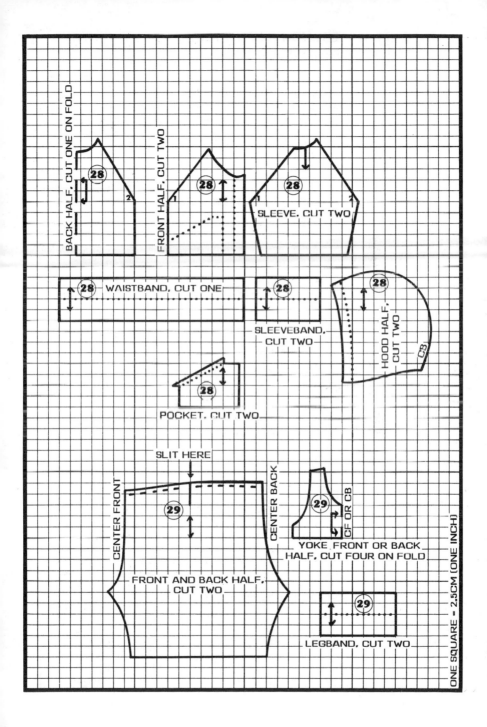

BACK HALF, CUT ONE ON FOLD

FRONT HALF, CUT TWO

SLEEVE, CUT TWO

WAISTBAND, CUT ONE

SLEEVEBAND, CUT TWO

HOOD HALF, CUT TWO

POCKET, CUT TWO

SLIT HERE

CENTER FRONT

CENTER BACK

YOKE FRONT OR BACK HALF, CUT FOUR ON FOLD

CF OR CB

FRONT AND BACK HALF, CUT TWO

LEGBAND, CUT TWO

ONE SQUARE = 2.5CM (ONE INCH)

30. SUMMER DRESS
Size: 6 months

Two rows of ruffled tiers gathered to bodice, self stretch binding.

Stretch fabrics only for bodice: Cotton knits. (Consider making bodice and each tier in different solid colors for a pretty effect. Make panties #31 to match.) **For tiers:** Cotton, seersucker, eyelet, cotton knits. **Fabric required:** Bodice – 25x90cm (1/4ydx36"); tiers – 25x90cm (1/4ydx36").

Sewing: Stitch left shoulder seam. Bind neck edge with bifold stretch tape made of self fabric (see page 35). Stitch right shoulder seam. Bind armholes with bifold stretch tape. Stitch side seams. Stitch each tier into a circle. Gather upper edge of upper tier and stitch it to bodice. Gather upper edge of lower tier and stitch it to upper tier. Hem lower edge narrowly.

31. PRETTY PANTIES
Size: 6 months

Little stretch panties with rib knit bands around legholes for snug fit to cover the diaper. Elasticized waist. Optional lace or eyelet trim or ruffle across back.

Stretch fabrics only: Cotton knits, stretch terry, velour. **Fabric required:** 50x90cm (20x36"), makes two panties. **Notions:** Elastic for waist, rib knit. Optional lace or eyelet (or bias strip made of self fabric) for ruffle at back.

Sewing: Stitch side seams. Stitch rib knit bands to legholes. Sew waist edge down to form a casing and insert elastic. (Optional: Before stitching side seams, stitch ruffled lace or eyelet ribbons, or narrowly hemmed gathered strip of self fabric, across panties back.)

32. T-SHIRT
Size: 6 months

Short or long raglan sleeves with rib knit bands, round neck opening with rib knit band.

Stretch fabrics only: Cotton knits, stretch terry, velour. **Fabric required:** 50x90cm (20x36"). **Notions:** Rib knit.

Sewing: Stitch sleeves to armhole edges of front and back. Stitch sides and underarms. Stitch rib knit bands around neck and sleeve ends. Overlock lower edge, press it under and topstitch in place.

Press trims and fabrics with raised design or nap from the wrong side over a soft terry towel to retain their three-dimensional appearance.

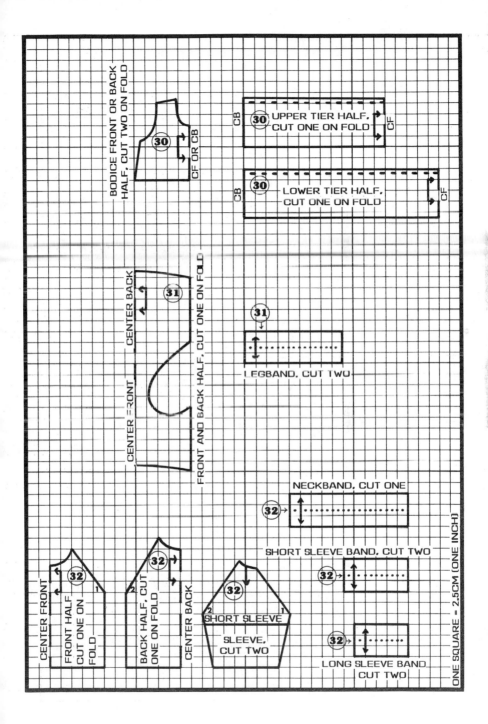

BODICE FRONT OR BACK HALF, CUT TWO ON FOLD

CF OR CB

(30)

(30) UPPER TIER HALF, CUT ONE ON FOLD

CB

CF

(30) LOWER TIER HALF, CUT ONE ON FOLD

CB

CF

CENTER BACK

(31)

CENTER FRONT

FRONT AND BACK HALF, CUT ONE ON FOLD

(31)

LEGBAND, CUT TWO

NECKBAND, CUT ONE

(32)

SHORT SLEEVE BAND, CUT TWO

(32)

(32) FRONT HALF CUT ONE ON FOLD

CENTER FRONT

1

(32) BACK HALF, CUT ONE ON FOLD

CENTER BACK

(32) SHORT SLEEVE

SLEEVE, CUT TWO

2

1

(32) LONG SLEEVE BAND, CUT TWO

ONE SQUARE = 2.5CM (ONE INCH)

87

33. JUMPSUIT (or romper)
Size: 6 months

Loose-fitting pants without side seams gathered to front bib (bib could be quilted), elasticized back edge. Shoulder straps with buttons. Elasticized ankles. (When too short, make pull-on pants or romper with elasticized legholes.)
Suggested fabrics: Cotton and blends, seersucker, eyelet, pinwale corduroy, cotton knits, fleece, velour. **Fabric required:** 50x115cm (½ydx45"). **Notions:** Two buttons for straps, elastic, two buttons (or snap fasteners or four ribbons) for side slits, doublefold bias tape.

Sewing: Stitch center back seam. Slit sides 5cm (2") from waist down (as shown in the pattern), bind slit edges with bias tape. On inside, zigzag stretched elastic to upper back edge, turn the elasticized edge under and edgestitch in place. Stitch center front seam. Prepare straps and stitch the raw ends to pants back under the elasticized edge. Stitch two bib sections together at top and sides (sew an appliqué onto bib if desired), clip curves, turn right side out and press. Gather upper edge of pants front and stitch it to the bib. Make buttonholes to bib and sew on buttons to strap ends. Add buttonholes and buttons (or snap fasteners or tie-on ribbons) for closing side slits. Stitch inner leg seams. Sew casings in leg ends and insert elastic. (Romper has elasticized leg ends.)

34. SLEEPER OR PLAYSUIT
Size: 6 months

Sleeve tops gathered to armholes, elasticized wrists forming self ruffles. Ruffle around neck. A slit with button closure at back. No side seams. Elasticized mid-back. Easy pleats for heels. Snap closure at inner leg seams. Lace trim.
Stretch fabrics only: Cotton knits, stretch terry, velour. (Flame-retardant fabrics are required by law on children's sleepwear.) **Fabric required:** 1mx115cm (1ydx45"). **Notions:** Elastic, lace, one button for back slit, snap fastener tape for inner leg seam.

Sewing: Stitch center front seam. Stitch center back seam leaving 5cm (2") open at neck. Stitch sides of neck opening under. Stitch shoulder seams. Trim sleeve ends with lace. On inside, zigzag stretched elastic around wrists about 5cm (2") from lower ends forming self ruffles. Stitch underarms. Gather sleeve tops and stitch sleeves to armholes. Trim outer edge and both short ends of neck ruffle with lace, gather upper edge and stitch the ruffle around the neck. Bind raw neck edge with unifold stretch tape made of self fabric (see page 35). On inside, stitch stretched elastic across back waist. Make pleats for heels (see #18). Stitch the seam around leg ends up to where seam allowances for inner legs begin. Sew on snap fastener tape for inner leg seam closure. Sew on button and loop for neck closure.

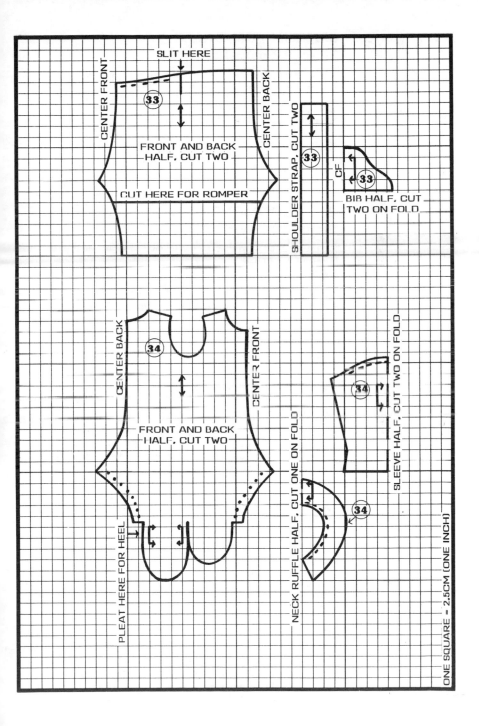

SLIT HERE

CENTER FRONT

(33)

FRONT AND BACK
HALF, CUT TWO

CUT HERE FOR ROMPER

CENTER BACK

SHOULDER STRAP, CUT TWO

(33)

CF

(33)

BIB HALF, CUT
TWO ON FOLD

CENTER BACK

(34)

FRONT AND BACK
HALF, CUT TWO

CENTER FRONT

SLEEVE HALF, CUT TWO ON FOLD

(34)

PLEAT HERE FOR HEEL

NECK RUFFLE HALF, CUT ONE ON FOLD

(34)

ONE SQUARE = 2.5CM (ONE INCH)

89

35. SUMMER DRESS
Size: 12 months

Sweet little dress. Shirred shoulder straps forming butterfly sleeves are stitched to shirred upper edge.
Suggested fabrics: Lightweight cotton types, batiste, seersucker, eyelet. **Fabric required:** 1mx115cm (1ydx45").
Notions: Elastic thread for shirring.

Sewing: Narrowly hem rounded sleeve ends. Stitch several rows of elastic shirring along shoulder strap area of sleeves and across upper edge of front and back. Stitch center back seam. Stitch shoulder straps under top edge of front and back. Hem lower edge of dress.

36. BLOOMERS
Size: 12 months

Puffed panties with elasticized waist and legholes.
Suggested fabrics: Same fabrics as for dress #35. **Fabric required:** 35x115cm (14x45"). **Notions:** Elastic.

Sewing: Stitch center back and center front seams. Stitch inner leg seams. Sew casings in waist and leghole edges and insert elastic.

37. PUFFED SUN BONNET
Size: 12 months

Puffed headpiece gathered to brim. Tie-on ribbons.
Suggested fabrics: Same fabrics as for dress #35. **Fabric required:** 50x90cm (½ydx36"). **Notions:** Elastic, interfacing, ribbons (two 25cm or 10" long each) for ties.

Sewing: Iron fusible interfacing to wrong side of one brim section. Stitch brims together, turn right side out, press. Sew a narrow casing in straight edge of headpiece, insert a piece of 10cm (4") long elastic (stitch elastic ends securely to casing ends). Gather rounded edge and stitch it to brim. Attach ribbons.

38. JUMPSUIT
Size: 12 months

Loose-fitting cute jumpsuit, buttoned front, long sleeves, rib knit bands, baggy pants gathered to bodice at waistline. Tapered leg ends to roll up.
Suggested fabrics: Fleece, velour, cotton knits, crinkly cotton. **Fabric required:** 1mx115cm (1ydx45"). **Notions:** Rib knit, four buttons (or snap fastener tape).

Sewing: Stitch shoulder seams. Stitch sleeves to armholes. Stitch sides and underarms. Overlock front edges, press them under, baste lower ends together overlapping 2½cm (1"). Stitch side seams of pants, inner leg seams, center front and center back seams. Gather upper edge of pants and stitch it to bodice. Stitch rib knit bands to sleeve ends and neck edge. Overlock leg ends, press them under narrowly, topstitch in place. Make buttonholes and sew on buttons (or snap fastener tape) for front closure.

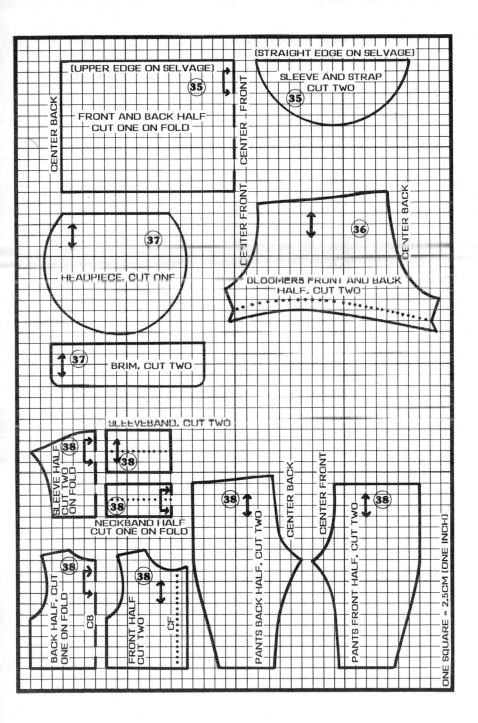

(STRAIGHT EDGE ON SELVAGE)

[UPPER EDGE ON SELVAGE]

CENTER BACK

35

SLEEVE AND STRAP
CUT TWO
35

FRONT AND BACK HALF
CUT ONE ON FOLD

CENTER FRONT

CENTER FRONT

36

CENTER BACK

37

HEADPIECE, CUT ONE

BLOOMERS FRONT AND BACK
HALF, CUT TWO

37

BRIM, CUT TWO

SLEEVEBAND, CUT TWO

38

38

SLEEVE HALF
CUT TWO
ON FOLD

38

NECKBAND HALF
CUT ONE ON FOLD

38

CENTER BACK

CENTER FRONT

38

ONE SQUARE = 2.5CM (ONE INCH)

38

BACK HALF, CUT
ONE ON FOLD

CB

38

FRONT HALF
CUT TWO

CF

PANTS BACK HALF, CUT TWO

PANTS FRONT HALF, CUT TWO

91

39. BODYSUIT
Size: 12 months

Simple design with facings around legholes, self stretch binding around all upper edges, buttons and buttonholes for shoulder closure. Very comfortable in hot weather around the clock.
Stretch fabrics only: Cotton knits, stretch terry, velour.
Fabric required: 1mx90cm (1ydx36"), makes two bodysuits.
Notions: Two buttons.

Sewing: Overlock outer edge of each facing. Stitch facings around legholes. Stitch sides and facing ends. Turn facings to inside and topstitch them in place. Bind raw upper edges (shoulders, neck and underarms) with unifold stretch tape made of self fabric or contrasting fabric (see page 35). Add buttons and buttonholes.

40. SUN BONNET
Size: 12 months

Elasticized back edge, tie-on ribbons.
Suggested fabrics: Lightweight cotton types, batiste, seersucker, calico, eyelet. **Fabric required:** 30x90cm (1/3ydx45"). **Notions:** Elastic, interfacing, two ribbons (25cm or 8" long each, or make your own ribbons).

Sewing: Iron fusible interfacing (two layers if necessary) to the wrong side of one brim section. Stitch the brim layers together around outer edge, clip curves, turn right side out and press. Overlock one long edge of headpiece, press it under 1.3cm (½") and edgestitch closed, forming a casing. Insert a piece of elastic (14cm or 5½" long) through casing, and attach elastic securely to casing ends. Bring both ends of elasticized casing together (but not overlapping). Bind entire raw neck edge with doublefold bias tape made of self fabric (see page 35). Stitch brim to headpiece. Attach ribbons.

41. SUMMER DRESS (jumper, nightie)
Size: 12 months

Loose-fitting design has front and back gathered to bias binding that extend into tie ends. Underarms bound with bias binding.
Suggested fabrics: Cotton types, flannelette, seersucker, eyelet, batiste, calico, broadcloth, cotton knits. (Flame-retardant fabrics are required by law on children's sleepwear.) **Fabric required:** 50x115cm (½ydx45"). **Notions:** Doublefold bias tape.

Sewing: Stitch side seams. Bind underarms with bias tape. Gather upper edges of front and back until they are 13cm (5") long each. Stitch bias tape (two 66cm or 26" long each) to gathered upper edges of front and back, centering tapes at center front and back and leaving tie ends extending at each side, edgestitch from end to end. Hem the lower edge of dress narrowly.

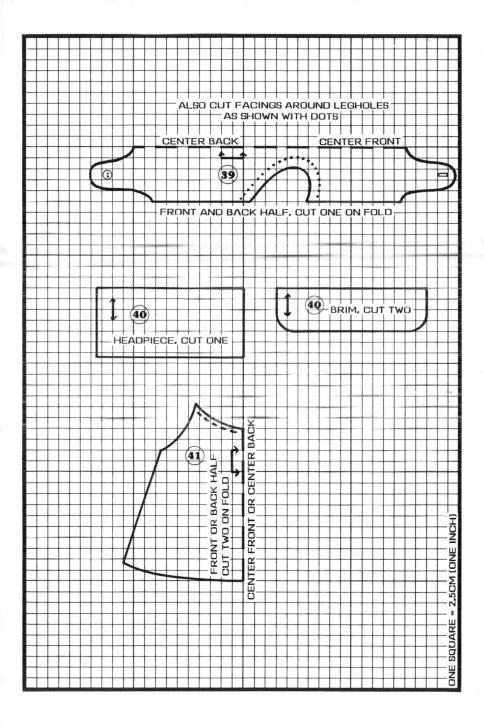

ALSO CUT FACINGS AROUND LEGHOLES
AS SHOWN WITH DOTS

CENTER BACK   CENTER FRONT

39

FRONT AND BACK HALF, CUT ONE ON FOLD

40

HEADPIECE, CUT ONE

40   BRIM, CUT TWO

41

FRONT OR BACK HALF
CUT TWO ON FOLD

CENTER FRONT OR CENTER BACK

ONE SQUARE = 2.5CM (ONE INCH)

42. TOP
Size: 12 months

Short or long raglan sleeves, rib knit bands around neck, sleeve ends and waist.
Stretch fabrics only: Cotton knits, stretch terry, velour. **Fabric required:** 30x115cm (1/3ydx45"). **Notions:** Rib knit.

Sewing: Stitch sleeves to armhole edges of front and back. Stitch sides and underarms. Stitch rib knit bands to neck opening, sleeve ends and lower edge.

43. HOODED JACKET (coat, bathrobe)
44. OVERALLS
Size: 12 months

Jacket: Loose-fitting design with long sleeves, front button closure. Bias binding. Sleeve ends and hood front edge are turned up for a decorative effect matching the pocket tops. (When sleeves get too short, just unfold sleeve ends; when again too short, add rib knit sleevebands. Lengthen the pattern for a coat or bathrobe.) Overalls: Straight legs, zippered front. Buttoned shoulders. Leg ends turned up. Bias binding. (When too short, just unfold leg ends; when again too short, add rib knit legbands.)
Suggested fabrics: Lightweight, reversible quilted fabric. Or use corduroy, nylon, windproof and water repellent fabric. If you use non-reversible fabric, line entire outfit (or only pockets, hood, sleeve ends and leg ends) with fabric such as flannelette or terry. **Fabric required for jacket and overalls:** 160x115cm (1 3/4 yd x 45"). **Notions:** Four packages of extrawide doublefold bias tape, six buttons, 25cm (10") long zipper.

Sewing jacket: Bind raw upper edge of each pocket with bias tape (wide zigzag is neat and fast), turn the edge down on outside for 5cm (2"), pin or baste. Bind raw pocket edges with bias tape, topstitch pockets in place. Stitch shoulder seams. Stitch sleeves to armholes. Stitch sides and underarms. Stitch hood center panel between hood sides. Stitch hood to neck opening. Bind hood and sleeve end seam allowances (they will show) with bias tape. Bind raw sleeve ends, hood front, jacket front and lower edge with bias tape. Make buttonholes and sew on buttons. Turn sleeve ends and hood front edge to outside.
Sewing overalls: Stitch zipper in place. Stitch center front seam below zipper. Stitch center back seam. Stitch inner leg seams. Bind seam allowances of leg ends with bias tape. Bind armholes, strap ends, neck opening and leg ends with bias tape. Add buttons and buttonholes. Turn leg ends to outside.

When both sides of fabric look alike or almost, stick a piece of masking tape to wrong side of all pieces while cutting. Pull the tape off immediately after sewing. (Be sure not to iron on the tape.)

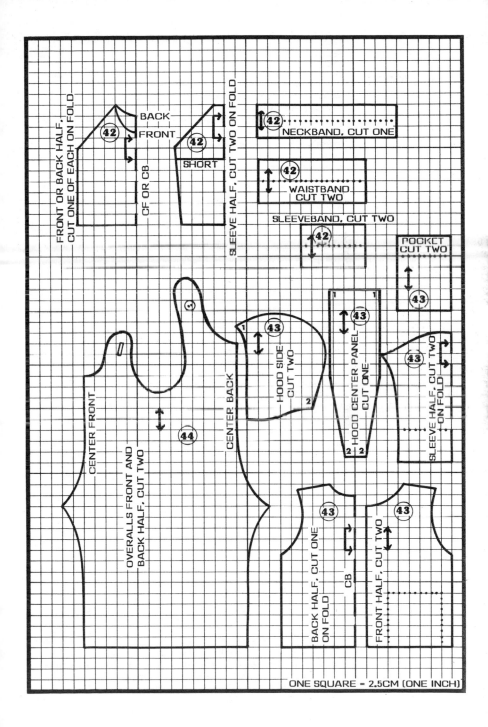

FRONT OR BACK HALF, CUT ONE OF EACH ON FOLD

BACK
FRONT

CF OR CB

SHORT

42

42

SLEEVE HALF, CUT TWO ON FOLD

42 NECKBAND, CUT ONE

42 WAISTBAND CUT TWO

SLEEVEBAND, CUT TWO

42

POCKET CUT TWO

43

CENTER FRONT

OVERALLS FRONT AND BACK HALF, CUT TWO

44

CENTER BACK

HOOD SIDE CUT TWO

43

1

2

HOOD CENTER PANEL CUT ONE

1 1

43

2 2

43 SLEEVE HALF, CUT TWO ON FOLD

BACK HALF, CUT ONE ON FOLD

43

CB

FRONT HALF, CUT TWO

43

ONE SQUARE = 2.5CM (ONE INCH)

45. PLAYSUIT OR SLEEPER
Size: 12 months

Self stretch binding, buttons and buttonholes on shoulder flaps. (When too short, or when your baby begins to walk and soles might become too slippery on uncarpeted floors, cut feet off and sew rib knit bands to leg ends. When again too short, cut off at underarms and make it into pull-on pants with elasticized waist.)
Stretch fabrics only: Cotton knits, stretch terry, velour. (Flame-retardant fabrics are required by law on children's sleepwear.) **Fabric required:** 1mx90cm (1ydx36"). **Notions:** Two buttons.

Sewing: Stitch half of the crotch piece between the legs of back piece. Stitch back seam of each sole to leg ends of back piece, matching numbers. Stitch sides and inner leg seams, connecting at the same time sole fronts and the crotch front. Bind raw edges of underarms-shoulders-neck with bifold stretch tape made of self fabric (see page 35). Add buttons and buttonholes.

46. SAILOR SUIT
Size: 12 months

Short sleeves with contrasting bands, zippered front, snap closure at crotch. White sailor collar with contrasting ribbon trim, contrasting tie.
Suggested fabrics: Cotton types, seersucker, cotton knits, velour. **Fabric required:** Front and back, sleeves and tabs (blue-white striped fabric) – 70x90cm (3/4 ydx45"); collar and sleeve bands (white fabric) – 30x90cm (12x36"); tie (red fabric) – 10x90cm (4x36"). **Notions:** 25cm (10") long zipper, blue rickrack for collar, 4 small buttons.

Sewing: Stitch center back seam. Stitch zipper in place. Stitch center front seam below zipper. Stitch shoulder seams. Press sleevebands in half right side out and stitch them to sleeve ends. Stitch sleeves to armholes. Fold each tab in half along dotted line, stitch sides and pointy ends, trim, turn right side out and press. Pin or baste tabs at each side of front waist (raw tab end even with raw side edge). Stitch sides and underarms catching in tab ends at the same time. Stitch rickrack along sides and straight back edge of one collar layer (about 2½cm or 1" in from edges). Stitch collar layers together at sides and back, trim corners, turn right side out and press. Right side of collar against wrong side of garment, stitch the collar around neck opening, clip curves, turn the collar to outside. Fold the tie in half lengthwise and stitch ends and side closed, leaving an opening, trim corners, turn right side out, slipstitch opening closed and press; tie it around the neck under the collar. Press under 2cm (3/4") along crotch edges at front and back, topstitch the folded edges closed. Overlock leg ends, press them under and topstitch in place. Add buttons and buttonholes for crotch closure. Add buttons to fasten tab ends to front sides of garment.

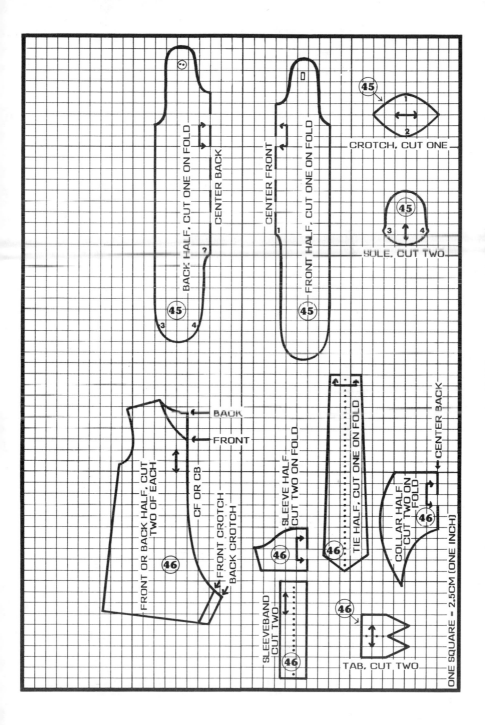

CROTCH, CUT ONE

SOLE, CUT TWO

BACK HALF, CUT ONE ON FOLD

CENTER BACK

CENTER FRONT

FRONT HALF, CUT ONE ON FOLD

BACK

FRONT

CF OR CB

FRONT OR BACK HALF, CUT TWO OF EACH

FRONT CROTCH

BACK CROTCH

SLEEVE HALF CUT TWO ON FOLD

SLEEVEBAND CUT TWO

TIE HALF, CUT ONE ON FOLD

CENTER BACK

COLLAR HALF CUT TWO ON FOLD

TAB, CUT TWO

ONE SQUARE = 2.5CM (ONE INCH)

97

47. JUMPER
Size: 12 months

Loose-fitting skirt gathered to yoke front and back (yoke can be quilted). Bias binding around armholes and neck opening. Back slit with button closure.
Suggested fabrics: Cotton types, seersucker, corduroy, eyelet, embroidered cotton, calico, broadcloth, cotton knits, velour, fleece. **Fabric required:** 60x115cm (2/3ydx45"). **Notions:** Doublefold bias tape, one button.

Sewing: If you wish to quilt the yoke, cut two layers of both front and back yoke, and quilt each two layers together (with an extra layer of soft fabric such as fleece in between). Gather upper edges of front and back skirt and stitch them to yoke. Stitch shoulder seams. Slit center back from neck down 6½cm (2½"), bind raw edges of slit with bias tape. Bind neck opening and armholes with bias tape. Stitch side seams. Overlock lower edge, press it under and topstitch in place. Sew on button and loop for back slit closure.

48. DRESS (or nightgown)
Size: 12 months

Front and back gathered to double-layered rib knit yoke, puffed short sleeves with rib knit bands. (Lengthen the pattern for a nightgown)
Suggested fabrics: Cotton types, seersucker, flannelette, corduroy, calico, broadcloth, cotton knits, velour, fleece. **Fabric required:** 60x115cm (2/3ydx45"). **Notions:** Rib knit for yoke and sleevebands.

Sewing: Stitch yokes together at shoulder seams (right sides in) for 4cm (1½") in from outside edges toward neck (shown with dots in the pattern); lock each end of stitching line securely. Fold yokes right side out so you have a neck opening in the middle, press. Gather upper edges of front and back and stitch them to yoke. Gather sleeve tops and stitch the sleeves to armholes. Stitch sides and underarms. Stitch rib knit bands to sleeve ends. Overlock lower edge, press it under and topstitch in place.

Don't buy fabrics **printed off-grain** since they are impossible to correct. Fabrics that are **pressed off-grain**, can be straightened by dampening and stretching on the bias; press if necessary.

When you stop your sewing machine to rearrange the fabric, leave the needle down so the stitching line doesn't shift.

Don't fold fusible interfacing or webbing; roll up leftover pieces into empty cardboard tubes from paper towels, aluminum foil, etc.

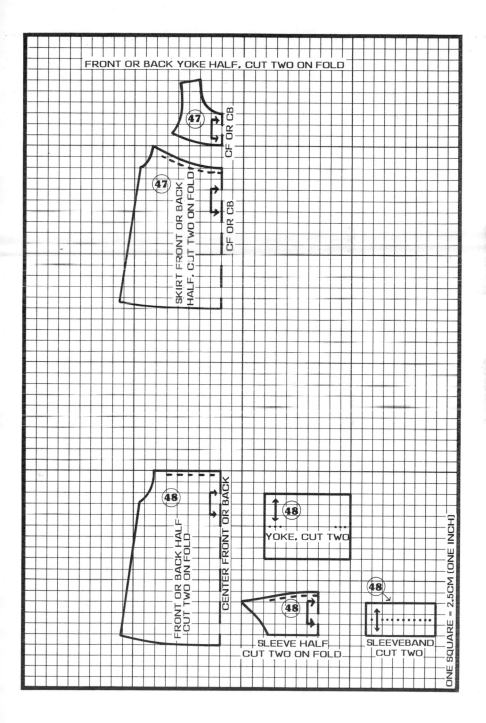

FRONT OR BACK YOKE HALF, CUT TWO ON FOLD

(47)

CF OR CB

(47)

SKIRT FRONT OR BACK
HALF, CUT TWO ON FOLD

CF OR CB

(48)

FRONT OR BACK HALF
CUT TWO ON FOLD

CENTER FRONT OR BACK

(48)

YOKE, CUT TWO

(48)

SLEEVE HALF
CUT TWO ON FOLD

(48)

SLEEVEBAND
CUT TWO

ONE SQUARE = 2.5CM (ONE INCH)

49. PULL-ON PANTS (or pajama pants)
Size: 12 months

Easy fit without side seams. Elasticized waist, rib knit legbands. (If long enough without rib knit legbands, stitch casings with elastic in leg ends and lenghten the pants later with rib knit bands. When again too short, make them into a pair of shorts. Make a top #42 to go with these pants as pajamas.)
Suggested fabrics: Cotton knits, stretch terry, velour, fleece. **Fabric required:** 50x90cm (½ydx36"). **Notions:** Elastic for waist, rib knit.

Sewing: Stitch center back and center front seams. Stitch inner leg seams. Stitch casing in waist edge and insert elastic. Stitch rib knit bands to leg ends.

50. JACKET
Size: 12 months

Hooded jacket with drawstrings through hood and hem casings, raglan sleeves, zippered front, kangaroo pockets, elasticized sleeve ends. (When too short, extend the sleeves and lower edge with rib knit bands.)
Stretch fabrics only: Mediumweight cotton knits, synthetic knits, stretch terry, velour. Also fleece. **Fabric required:** 70x115cm (3/4ydx45"). **Notions:** Elastic, cord for hood and hem casings, separating 30cm (12") long zipper.

Sewing: Overlock bias edge of each pocket and stitch them under, press upper edge and longer side under and topstitch pockets in place (as shown in the pattern). Stitch sleeves to armhole edges of front and back. Stitch sides and underarms. Stitch hood center back seam. Press under 2½cm (1") along hood front edge (turn lower ends of casing allowance under on the bias) and stitch close to edge, forming a casing. Press front edges under 1.3cm (½") as shown in the pattern. Sew zipper in place. Stitch hood to neck edge. Sew casings in sleeve ends and insert elastic. Sew lower edge under into a casing and insert cord. Insert cord through hood casing. Catch cords at center back of hood and hem casings with a few stitches through all thicknesses so they won't slip out.

Cut folded fabric with right sides together whenever possible so center seams are ready to stitch together.

Make a no-cost embroidery hoop from a large plastic container with tight-fitting lid. Cut off and discard both the center of lid and the entire container below rim. Snap the remaining rims together like a hoop.

To avoid puckers, never glide the iron when applying fusible interfacing.

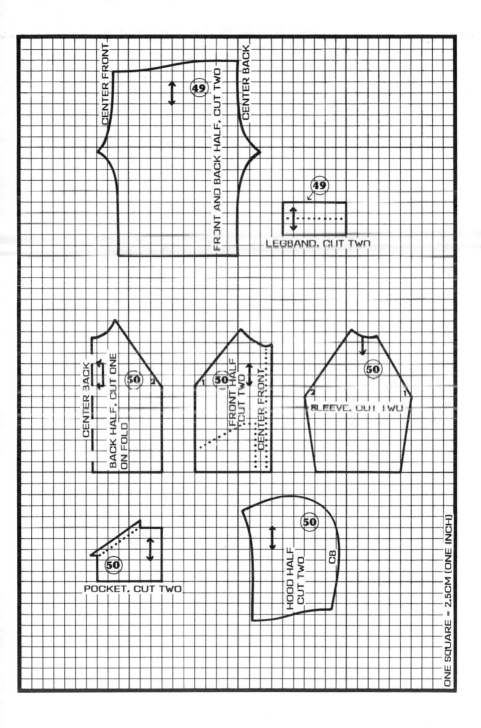

CENTER FRONT

49

FRONT AND BACK HALF, CUT TWO

CENTER BACK

49

LEGBAND, CUT TWO

CENTER BACK

50   2

BACK HALF, CUT ONE
ON FOLD

1   50

FRONT HALF
CUT TWO

CENTER FRONT

50

2   1

SLEEVE, CUT TWO

50

POCKET, CUT TWO

50

HOOD HALF
CUT TWO

CB

ONE SQUARE = 2.5CM (ONE INCH)

51. SWEATSHIRT (or pajama top) OR MINIDRESS
Size: 24 months

Sweatshirt has raglan sleeves, rib knit around sleeve ends, neck and waist. (Optional: Add hood and kangaroo pocket if desired.) Dress is the same as sweatshirt except for the waistband which is single-layered with ruffled skirt gathered to it. (Or trim off a bit from each of the four raglan edges and stitch single-layered rib knit between sleeves and bodice.)
Stretch fabrics only: Velour, stretch terry, cotton or blended knits. Also fleece. **Fabric required:** Sweatshirt – 50x115cm (½ydx45"); dress – 55x115cm (22x45"). **Notions:** Rib knit.

Sewing sweatshirt: Monogram child's name or sew an appliqué onto front if desired. Stitch sleeves to armhole edges of front and back. Stitch sides and underarms. Stitch rib knit bands to sleeve ends, neck and lower edge.
Sewing minidress: Sew as sweatshirt except for the waistband. Stitch short ends of waistband together into a circle. Try the band on your child and adjust if necessary (it should fit snugly just around the hips). Stitch upper edge of single-layered band to upper bodice. Stitch skirt side seam, gather upper edge and stitch it to lower edge of waistband. Overlock lower edge of minidress, press it under and topstitch in place.

52. PULL-ON PANTS (or pajama pants)
Size: 24 months

Easy fit without side seams. Elasticized waist, rib knit legbands. (If long enough without legbands, stitch elasticized casings in leg ends and lengthen them later with rib knit legbands. When too short, make them into a pair of shorts. Make a pair to team up with top #51 for pajamas.)
Stretch fabrics only: Velour, stretch terry, cotton knits. Also fleece. **Fabric required:** 60x90cm (2/3ydx32"). **Notions:** Elastic for waist, rib knit.

Sewing: Stitch center back and center front seams. Stitch inner leg seams. Stitch casing in waist edge and insert elastic. Stitch rib knit bands to leg ends.

Need piping trim? Try encasing cord or yarn by sewing bias tape around it.

Trim mesh garment's hem with bias tape instead of turning it under. For seams in mesh with very big holes, sew narrow seams from right side of garment, and cover them with doublefold bias tape.

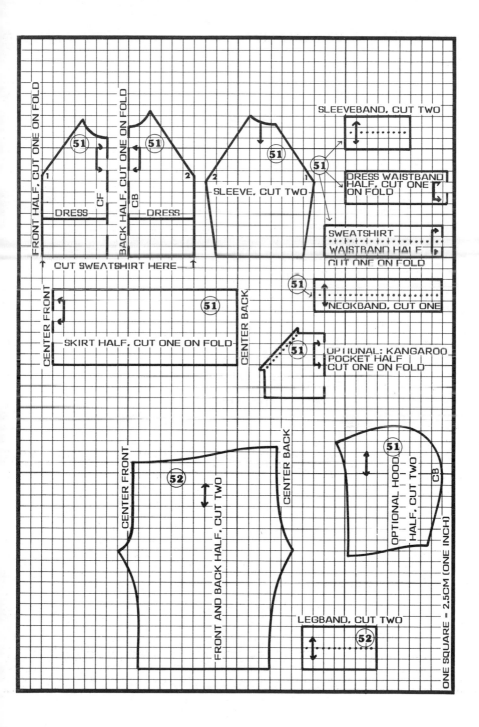

FRONT HALF, CUT ONE ON FOLD

51

1 CF 1

DRESS

BACK HALF, CUT ONE ON FOLD

51

CB

DRESS

2

SLEEVE, CUT TWO

51

2 1

SLEEVEBAND, CUT TWO

51

DRESS WAISTBAND
HALF, CUT ONE
ON FOLD

51

SWEATSHIRT
WAISTBAND HALF
CUT ONE ON FOLD

↑ CUT SWEATSHIRT HERE ↑

CENTER FRONT

SKIRT HALF, CUT ONE ON FOLD

51

CENTER BACK

51

NECKBAND, CUT ONE

51

OPTIONAL: KANGAROO
POCKET HALF
CUT ONE ON FOLD

CENTER FRONT

52

FRONT AND BACK HALF, CUT TWO

CENTER BACK

51

OPTIONAL HOOD
HALF, CUT TWO

CB

LEGBAND, CUT TWO

52

ONE SQUARE = 2.5CM (ONE INCH)

53. DRESS
Size: 24 months

Puffed short or long sleeves, elasticized sleeve ends, button back closure and long ribbons to tie at waist back. Make bloomers #54 to match.
Suggested fabrics: Lightweight cotton, seersucker, calico, broadcloth, eyelet, pinwale corduroy, cotton knits, fleece.
Fabric required: 1mx115cm (1ydx45"). **Notions:** Two small buttons, narrow elastic for sleeve ends.

Sewing: Stitch shoulder seams. Stitch front facing to back facing allowances at shoulder seams. Turn facing wrong side out and stitch it in place all around the neck, clip curves, overlock outer edge, turn facing to inside and press. Stitch facing to shoulder seams (stitch-in-ditch). Stitch center back seam from hem up to where opening in back facing begins. Topstitch around neck and along back opening, 6mm (1/4") from the edge, to prevent rolling. Gather sleeve tops and stitch the sleeves to armholes. On inside, stitch stretched elastic to sleeve ends, turn the elasticized edges under and edgestitch them in place. To make the ribbons, fold each strip in half lengthwise and stitch long edge closed, turn right side out and press; tuck one raw end of each ribbon to inside and slipstitch in place. Stitch sides and underarms sandwiching the raw ribbon ends in the side seams at the same time. Tie ribbons at back. Overlock lower edge of dress, press it under and topstitch in place.

54. BLOOMERS
Size: 24 months

Puffed panties with elasticized waist and legholes to go with the dress or pinafore on this page.
Suggested fabrics: Same fabrics as for dress and pinafore.
Fabric required: 50x115cm (½ydx45"). **Notions:** Elastic for waist and legholes.

Sewing: See design #36.

55. PINAFORE
Size: 24 months

Pretty pinafore to use as a coverup or sundress. Make a pair of bloomers #54 to match. Pinafore has button back closure and lace or eyelet trim.
Suggested fabrics: Cotton types, seersucker, calico, broadcloth, batiste, eyelet. **Fabric required:** 50x115cm (½ydx45"). **Notions:** Two buttons, lace.

Sewing: Sew an appliqué onto front if desired. Stitch shoulder seams. Trim armholes with lace. Stitch side seams. Trim neck opening, lower edge and back edges with lace. Make buttonholes and sew on buttons for back closure.

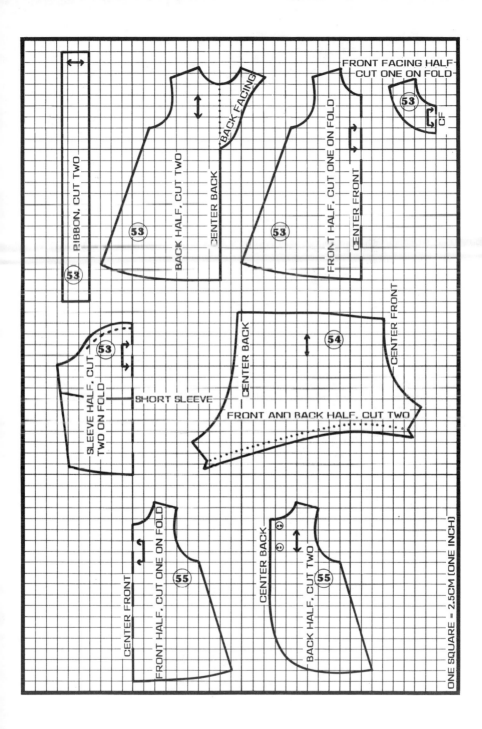

RIBBON, CUT TWO

(53)

BACK FACING

BACK HALF, CUT TWO

CENTER BACK

(53)

FRONT FACING HALF
CUT ONE ON FOLD

(53)

CF

FRONT HALF, CUT ONE ON FOLD

CENTER FRONT

(53)

CENTER FRONT

(54)

CENTER BACK

SHORT SLEEVE

SLEEVE HALF, CUT
TWO ON FOLD

(53)

FRONT AND BACK HALF, CUT TWO

CENTER FRONT

FRONT HALF, CUT ONE ON FOLD

(55)

CENTER BACK

BACK HALF, CUT TWO

(55)

ONE SQUARE = 2.5CM (ONE INCH)

56. V-NECK TOP
Size: 24 months

Short raglan sleeves, neckband, patch pocket on front. Make shorts #57 to match.
Stretch fabrics only: Stretch terry, velour, cotton knits. **Fabric required:** 50x115cm (½ydx45").

Sewing: Sew an appliqué onto pocket if desired. Prepare pocket and topstitch it in place. Stitch sleeves to armhole edges of front and back. Stitch sides and underarms. Overlock sleeve ends and lower edge, press them under and topstitch in place. Stitch neckband ends together into a circle, clip the seam allowance of V-point almost to the stitching line, fold the band in half lengthwise and press. Stitch the prepared band around neck opening, stretching slightly for neat fit, press.

57. SHORTS
Size: 24 months

Easy and comfortable design without side seams. Elasticized waist. Legbands provide snug fit to cover the diaper. Make V-neck shirt #56 to match.
Stretch fabrics only: Stretch terry, velour, rib knit, cotton knits. **Fabric required:** 50x90cm (½ydx36"). **Notions:** Wide elastic for waist.

Sewing: Stitch center front and center back seams. Stitch inner leg seams. Stitch bands to leg ends. Sew waist edge down into a casing and insert elastic.

Toddlers will give you sewing peace if you let them 'sew', too. Give the child a narrow shoe lace to thread through plastic canvas.

Easy shirring with no breakage: Zigzag wide stitches over, not through, cord (or buttonhole twist, strong nylon thread or dental floss). Attach one end securely, then gather the fabric by pulling the other end of the cord.

Cut tiny clips at each end of permanent foldline, remove pattern, separate fabric layers, fold each with wrong sides together along fold line, using clip marks as guides, and press.

106

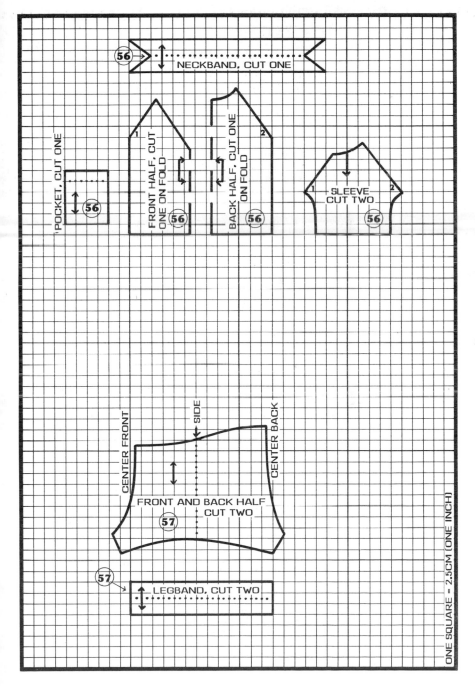

NECKBAND, CUT ONE

POCKET, CUT ONE

FRONT HALF, CUT ONE ON FOLD

BACK HALF, CUT ONE ON FOLD

SLEEVE CUT TWO

CENTER FRONT

SIDE

CENTER BACK

FRONT AND BACK HALF CUT TWO

LEGBAND, CUT TWO

ONE SQUARE = 2.5CM (ONE INCH)

107

58. PAJAMAS (or Bermuda shorts)
Size: 24 months

Loose-fitting top with short raglan sleeves, elasticized neck opening and sleeve ends. Pants without side seams have straight legs and elasticized waist casing. (When too short, extend leg ends with rib knit bands or cut them into knee-high pants.)
Suggested fabrics: Lightweight cotton types, flannelette, seersucker, batiste, cotton knits. (Flame-retardant fabrics are required by law on children's sleepwear.) **Fabric required:** 140x115cm (1½ydx45"). **Notions:** Wide elastic for waist, narrow elastic for sleeve ends and neck opening.

Sewing pajama top: Stitch sleeves to armhole edges of front and back. Stitch sides and underarms. Overlock sleeve ends and neck opening, stitch them down into casings, insert elastic. Overlock lower edge, press it under and topstitch in place.

Sewing pajama pants: Stitch center back and center front seams. Stitch inner leg seams. Overlock waist edge, stitch it down into a casing, insert elastic. Overlock leg ends, press them under and topstitch in place.

59. TANK TOP (or dress)
Size: 24 months

Simple sleeveless top, self stretch binding. (Add ruffle to lower edge for a minidress. Enlarge pattern size #31 to make a pair of matching panties.)
Stretch fabrics only: Cotton knits, stretch terry, velour, rib knit (enlarge pattern slightly if you use non-stretch mesh). **Fabric required:** 50x90cm (½ydx36"), makes two tops.

Sewing: Stitch left shoulder seam. Bind neck opening with bifold stretch tape made of self fabric (see page 35). Stitch right shoulder seam. Bind armholes with bifold stretch tape. Stitch side seams. Overlock lower edge, press it under and topstitch in place.

Reduce noise and prevent sliding by placing a rubber-backed carpet piece under your sewing machine. Get a suitable piece free from your local carpet dealer's discontinued samples. Another piece under foot-pedal will prevent it from sliding on uncarpeted floor.

Recycle transparent milk bags to store patterns and notions.

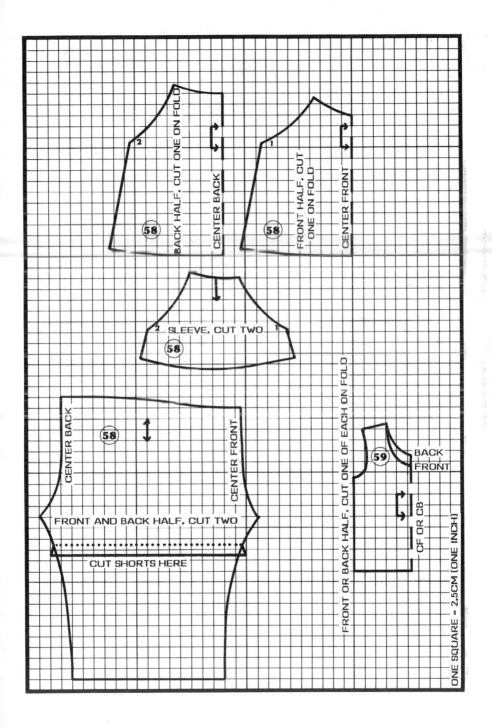

BACK HALF, CUT ONE ON FOLD

CENTER BACK

(58)

2

FRONT HALF, CUT ONE ON FOLD

CENTER FRONT

(58)

1

2 SLEEVE, CUT TWO 1

(58)

CENTER BACK

(58)

CENTER FRONT

FRONT AND BACK HALF, CUT TWO

CUT SHORTS HERE

FRONT OR BACK HALF, CUT ONE OF EACH ON FOLD

(59)

BACK

FRONT

CF OR CB

ONE SQUARE = 2.5CM (ONE INCH)

109

60. SUN ROMPER OR MAILLOT OR BODYSUIT
Size: 24 months

Facings around legholes. Elasticized self stretch binding.
Two-way stretch fabrics only: Spandex. **Fabric required:** 50x90cm (½ydx36"). **Notions:** Narrow swimsuit elastic.

Sewing: Stitch crotch reinforcement piece to the wrong side of garment. stitching all edges securely with stretch stitch. Stitch facings to legholes. Stitch sides and facing ends. Turn facings to inside and topstitch them in place with stretch stitch. On inside. zigzag gently stretched elastic to neck edges of front and back. Bind raw edges of armholes and elasticized neck opening with bifold stretch tape made of self fabric or contrasting fabric (see page 35). Stitch shoulder seams. [Variation shown in the pattern: Cut front section as shown in the pattern, add seam allowances. and sandwich the ruffle in this seam prior to sewing side seams.]

61. SWIMTRUNKS
Size: 24 months

Facings around legholes, elasticized waist casing.
Two-way stretch fabrics only: Spandex. **Fabric required:** 50x90cm (½ydx36"). **Notions:** Wide swimsuit elastic for waist.

Sewing: Stitch crotch reinforcement piece to the wrong side of garment. stitching all edges securely with stretch stitch. Stitch facings to legholes. Stitch sides and facing ends. Turn facings to inside and topstitch them in place around legholes with stretch stitch. Sew casing in waist edge and insert elastic.

62. CAP
Size: 24 months

Easy cap with brim, elasticized back edge.
Suggested fabrics: Mediumweight cotton types. denim, corduroy. **Fabric required:** 25x115cm (1/4ydx45"). **Notions:** Interfacing, elastic.

Sewing: Iron fusible interfacing to wrong side of one brim layer. Stitch brim layers together around curved outer seam, clip curves almost to the stitching line, turn right side out and press. Topstitch outer edge to prevent rolling. Stitch the four crown sections together. Stitch brim to crown. Stitch short ends of facing together into a circle, overlock outer edge. Right sides together, all raw edges even and brim in between, stitch the facing to lower edge of crown. Stitch a piece of stretched elastic (7½cm or 3" long) to the back edge seam allowance. stretching the elastic to its maximum length while sewing. Turn facing to inside and topstitch it in place around crown's lower edge.

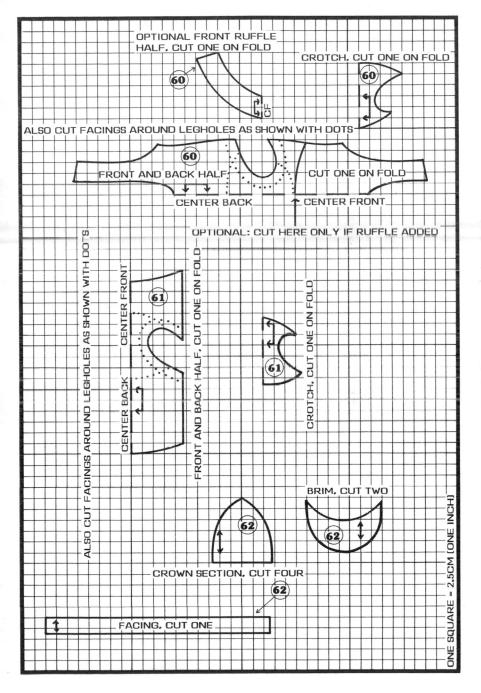

OPTIONAL FRONT RUFFLE HALF, CUT ONE ON FOLD

60

CROTCH, CUT ONE ON FOLD

60

CF

ALSO CUT FACINGS AROUND LEGHOLES AS SHOWN WITH DOTS

60

FRONT AND BACK HALF

CUT ONE ON FOLD

CENTER BACK

CENTER FRONT

OPTIONAL: CUT HERE ONLY IF RUFFLE ADDED

ALSO CUT FACINGS AROUND LEGHOLES AS SHOWN WITH DOTS

CENTER FRONT

61

CENTER BACK

FRONT AND BACK HALF, CUT ONE ON FOLD

61

CROTCH, CUT ONE ON FOLD

BRIM, CUT TWO

62

62

62

CROWN SECTION, CUT FOUR

62

FACING, CUT ONE

ONE SQUARE = 2.5CM (ONE INCH)

111

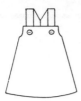

63. JUMPER
Size: 24 months

Loose-fitting simple jumper with back straps buttoned to front bib. Make a T-shirt #66 to go with this jumper. (When too short, it can still serve as a cover-up over dresses or blouses & pants. Or cut bib and straps off and make it into a skirt by adding a wide decorative elastic for a waistband.)

Suggested fabrics: Cotton types, corduroy, denim, seersucker, velour, fleece, lightweight quilted fabrics. **Fabric required:** 70x115cm (3/4ydx45"). **Notions:** 2 buttons.

Sewing: Stitch front facing in place around armholes and upper edge, trim corners and clip curves, turn the facing right side out and press it to inside. Stitch back facing in place around armholes and shoulder straps, clip curves and trim corners, turn the facing right side out and press it to inside. Open out facing ends at underarm edges, stitch side seams and facing ends. Press facings to inside and stitch them in place at side seams (stitch-in-ditch). Topstitch along entire upper edge and strap ends. Overlock lower edge of jumper, press it under and topstitch in place. Add buttons and buttonholes.

64. CARDIGAN
Size: 24 months

Easy one-piece pattern, pockets, front bands with buttons and buttonholes.

Stretch fabrics only: Velour, cotton knits, stretch terry, acrylic knits. Also fleece. **Fabric required:** 70x115cm (3/4 ydx45"). **Notions:** Four buttons.

Sewing: Overlock bias edge of each pocket and topstitch them under, press all raw edges under and topstitch the pockets in place. Clip seam allowances under arms until stitching line. In one continuous seam, stitch underarm and horizontal front seam at each side. Reinforce the seam with a second stitching line where underarm and horizontal front seams meet. Press front band in half lengthwise right side out and stitch it to front edges and around neck, stretching slightly for neat fit. Overlock sleeve ends and lower edge of cardigan, press them under and topstitch in place. Add buttons and buttonholes.

Tape a paper bag to sewing table's edge for quick scrap disposal.

Clean your overlock machine with a narrow bottle brush. Then vacuum through a narrow funnel that has extra long tip (tape on a piece of straw for extension if necessary), to get maximum suction.

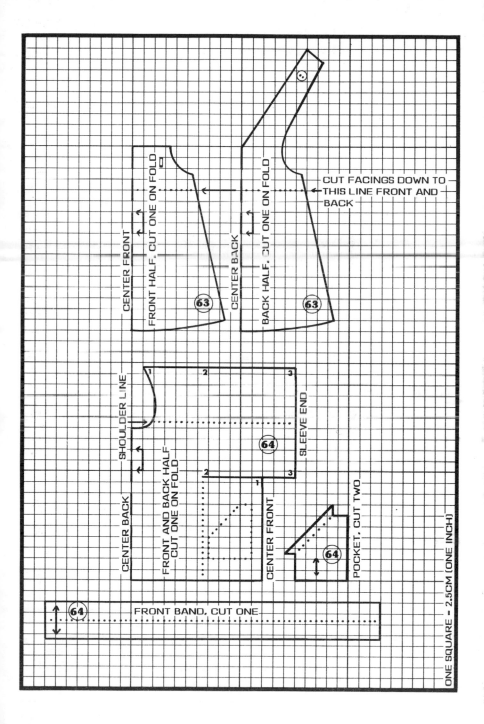

CUT FACINGS DOWN TO THIS LINE FRONT AND BACK

CENTER FRONT

FRONT HALF, CUT ONE ON FOLD

63

CENTER BACK

BACK HALF, CUT ONE ON FOLD

63

SHOULDER LINE

SLEEVE END

64

CENTER BACK

FRONT AND BACK HALF CUT ONE ON FOLD

CENTER FRONT

POCKET, CUT TWO

64

64

FRONT BAND, CUT ONE

ONE SQUARE = 2.5CM (ONE INCH)

113

65. OVERALLS
Size: 24 months

Loose-fitting straight-legged overalls without side seams.
Straps buttoned to front bib. Patch pockets. (When too
short, lengthen overalls by stitching rib knit bands to
leg ends. When again too short, make them into pull-
on pants with elasticized waist casing.)
Suggested fabrics: Corduroy, denim, mediumweight cotton
types, lightweight quilted fabrics. **Fabric required:**
120x115cm (1 1/4 yd x 45"). **Notions:** Two buttons.

Sewing: Stitch center front seam. Sew an appliqué onto
front or pockets if desired. Prepare pockets and topstitch
them in place. Stitch center front seam of facings (if
not cut on fold). Stitch facing to garment upper edge
including underarms and strap ends, clip curves and trim
corners, turn right side out and press the facing to inside.
Open out facing ends and stitch center back seam of
overalls and facing ends. Turn facing to inside and topstitch
in place along entire upper edge including underarms
and strap ends. Stitch facing to center back and center
front seams (stitch-in-ditch). Stitch inner leg seams.
Overlock leg ends, press them under and topstitch in
place. Add buttons and buttonholes.

66. T-SHIRT
Size: 24 months

Straight top with short or long sleeves, round neck, rib
knit bands around neck and sleeve ends.
Stretch fabrics only: Cotton knits, stretch terry, velour.
Fabric required: 50x115cm (½ydx45"). **Notions:** Rib knit.

Sewing: Stitch shoulder seams. Stitch sleeves to armholes.
Stitch sides and underarms. Stitch rib knit bands to sleeve
ends and neck opening. Overlock lower edge and stitch
it in place.

If you need to apply fusible interfacing, cut the fabric
piece first; then, using iron's tip, fuse a larger piece
of interfacing to center of fabric's wrong side. Trim
interfacing around fabric edges, press.

To make new from old, check if the fabric is reversible.
The wrong side might look like new even if right
side is worn, faded and linty.

Before you cut out expensive fabric or an unusual
pattern, test it first in inexpensive fabric.

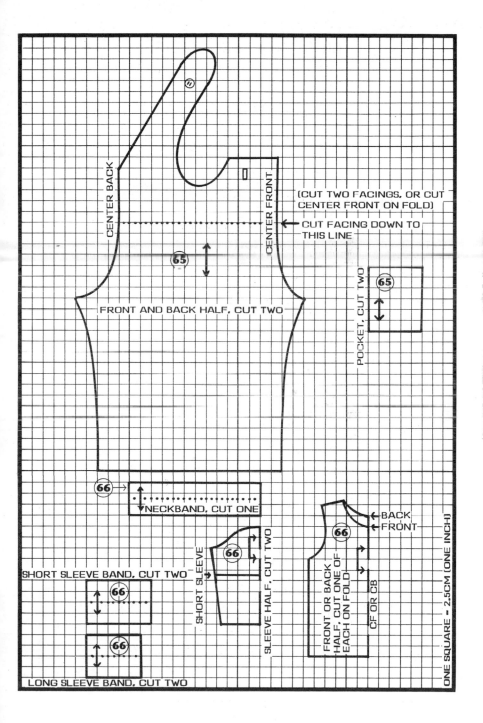

CENTER BACK

CENTER FRONT

(CUT TWO FACINGS, OR CUT
CENTER FRONT ON FOLD)

← CUT FACING DOWN TO
THIS LINE

65

FRONT AND BACK HALF, CUT TWO

POCKET, CUT TWO

65

66 →

NECKBAND, CUT ONE

← BACK
← FRONT

66

SHORT SLEEVE

66

SLEEVE HALF, CUT TWO

SHORT SLEEVE BAND, CUT TWO

66

66

LONG SLEEVE BAND, CUT TWO

FRONT OR BACK
HALF, CUT ONE OF
EACH ON FOLD

CF OR CB

ONE SQUARE = 2.5CM (ONE INCH)

115

67. TABARD
Size: 24 months

Loose-fitting apron/coverup to wear over other clothing. Bias binding around all raw edges including neck opening. Ties at each side.

Suggested fabrics: Tightly-woven cotton types, nylon, vinyl-coated fabrics. **Fabric required:** 1mx90cm (1ydx36").
Notions: Doublefold bias tape.

Sewing: Bind all raw edges with bias tape. Prepare four ribbons from doublefold bias tape (20 or 8" long each), edgestitching through all thicknesses from end to end. Stitch the ribbons to both sides of waist front and back. (Optional: Sew a pocket or appliqué onto front if desired.)

68. HOODED COAT (or bathrobe)
Size: 24 months

Loose-fitting unlined coat with long sleeves, drawstring hood, patch pockets and front button closure. (When too short, add rib knit waistband and sleevebands to make it a jacket. Lengthen the pattern for a bathrobe.)

Suggested fabrics: Corduroy, soft denim, quilted fabrics, mediumweight cotton types. (Terry, stretch terry or velour for a bathrobe.) **Fabric required:** 120x115cm (1 1/4 yd x 45"). **Notions:** Four buttons (or separating zipper), 90cm (1 yard) long cord, two press-on metal rings.

Sewing: Prepare pockets and topstitch them in place. Stitch shoulder seams. Stitch sleeves to armholes. Stitch sides and underarms. Stitch hood back seam. Press hood band in half lengthwise right side out. Open the band and press metal rings through both ends (as shown in the pattern); if you don't have rings, make buttonholes instead. Place a cord inside folded band and pull cord ends to right side through rings. Fold the band in half again and stitch it to hood front edge so that the metal rings are inside (be careful not to stitch through the cord). Overlock front edges, press facing allowances under, open them out and turn them to outside. Pin or baste the hood around the neck so that hood front edges are neatly sandwiched between the right side of fabric and the front facing allowances, all raw edges even, and stitch through all thicknesses. Turn facings to inside. Overlock lower edge and sleeve ends, press them under and topstitch in place. Add buttons and buttonholes (or separating zipper) for front closure.

Turn store-bought garments inside out to see how and in what order the seams are sewn. These fast, professional shortcuts are equally handy for home sewing too.

116

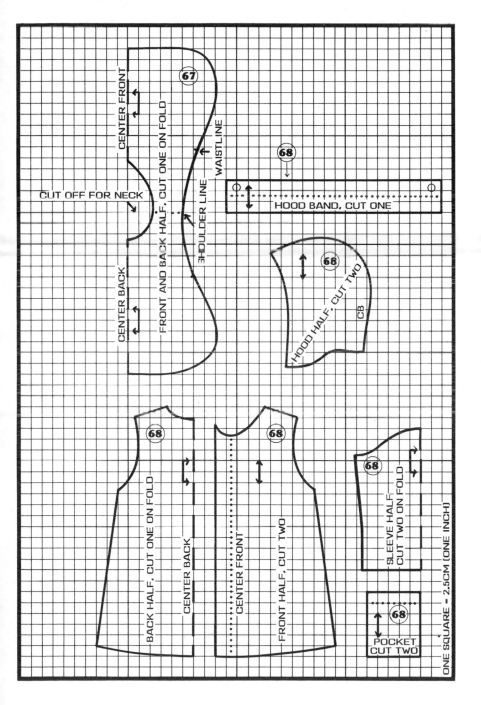

CENTER FRONT

67

CUT OFF FOR NECK

FRONT AND BACK HALF, CUT ONE ON FOLD

SHOULDER LINE

WAISTLINE

CENTER BACK

68

HOOD BAND, CUT ONE

68

HOOD HALF, CUT TWO

CB

68

BACK HALF, CUT ONE ON FOLD

CENTER BACK

68

CENTER FRONT

FRONT HALF, CUT TWO

68

SLEEVE HALF, CUT TWO ON FOLD

68

POCKET CUT TWO

ONE SQUARE – 2.5CM (ONE INCH)

117

69. COVERALLS AND BALACLAVA HELMET
Size: 24 months

Straight legs, zippered front, long sleeves, no side seams. Rib knit bands around sleeve ends, neck and leg ends. (When too short, remove the zipper and make them into pull-on pants.)
Suggested fabrics: Corduroy, soft denim, quilted fabrics, windproof and water resistant fabrics. Also fleece or velour. **Fabric required:** 120x115cm (1 1/4 ydx45"). **Notions:** 35cm (14") long zipper, rib knit. **Balaclava helmet:** Pattern and directions, see design #19.

Sewing: Sew zipper in place. Stitch center front seam below zipper. Stitch shoulder seams. Stitch underarms of sleeves, then stitch sleeves to armholes. Stitch center back seam. Stitch inner leg seams. Sew rib knit bands to sleeve ends and leg ends. Sew rib knit band to neck edge, pulling band ends downward to round the corners. (Optional: Stitch stretched elastic across mid-back.)

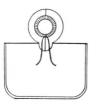

70. HOODED PONCHO
Size: 24 months

Drawstring hood, entire lower edge of poncho trimmed with bias binding or foldover braid.
Suggested fabrics: For a rain poncho, use vinyl, nylon, or other windproof and water repellent fabrics. For a warm coverup, use soft and warm fabrics such as wool duffle, corduroy, wool and blends, knits. For a beach coverup in summer, use absorbent fabrics such as terry, stretch terry, velour. **Fabric required:** 120x90cm (1 1/4 ydx36"). **Notions:** Rib knit for hood frontband, 110cm (43") long cord, doublefold bias tape or foldover braid (or make your own).

Sewing: Stitch center back and center front seams of hood. Press and stitch band ends under. Press the band in half lengthwise and stitch it to hood front edge, forming a casing and leaving ends open for cord. Stitch hood to neck opening. Bind entire lower edge with doublefold bias tape or foldover braid. Insert a cord through hood casing. Vinyl rain poncho: Pins will permanently mark the vinyl and may even tear it, so stick the pins in seam allowances only. When cutting out the vinyl, keep the layers from shifting by applying pieces of rolled-up adhesive tape or masking tape between the two layers. Use weights (such as books or canned foods) to hold the pattern in place, mark the cutting line with a crayon or marker. If you find it hard to sew vinyl, bind all seams with doublefold bias tape so that these decorative seams are on the right side of garment. "Appliqué" vinyl poncho easily with cut-out self-adhesive designs.

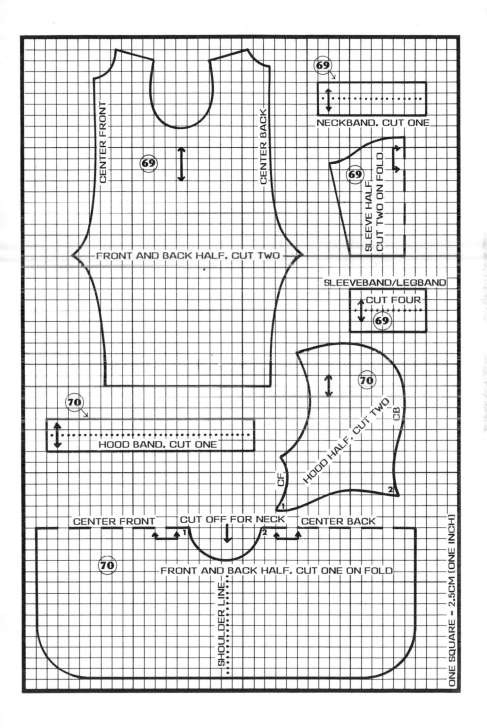

NECKBAND, CUT ONE

SLEEVE HALF
CUT TWO ON FOLD

SLEEVEBAND/LEGBAND
CUT FOUR

CENTER FRONT

CENTER BACK

FRONT AND BACK HALF, CUT TWO

HOOD HALF, CUT TWO

CB

CF

HOOD BAND, CUT ONE

CENTER FRONT   CUT OFF FOR NECK   CENTER BACK

FRONT AND BACK HALF, CUT ONE ON FOLD

SHOULDER LINE

ONE SQUARE = 2.5CM (ONE INCH)

BE A PART OF MY BOOKS

Realizing that some of the best ideas might come from my innovative readers, I am inviting your comments and suggestions.

If you have great sewing tips or other suitable ideas that you would like to share, I would love to hear from you. Should I use your idea in one of my books, I will send you a complimentary, autographed copy of that book. Write to: Leila Albala, ALPEL PUBLISHING, P.O.Box 203, Chambly, Quebec J3L 4B3, Canada.

NOTES _____

_____

_____

_____

_____

_____

_____

_____

_____

_____

_____

_____

MEASUREMENT CHART

For a handy reference, record here the measurements
of your child/children. Use a pencil for easy changes.

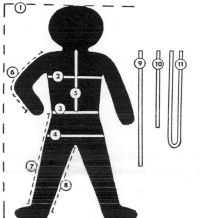

		Child's name Date	Child's name Date
1.	HEIGHT		
2.	CHEST		
3.	WAIST		
4.	HIPS		
5.	BACK WAIST LENGTH		
6.	LONG SLEEVE LENGTH		
7.	PANTS SIDE SEAM		
8.	PANTS INSEAM		
9.	DRESS LENGTH		
10.	T-SHIRT LENGTH		
11.	TRUNK (shoulder-to-shoulder- through-crotch, useful for maillot, bodysuit, coveralls)		

INDEX

GLIMPSES OF THE AUTHOR

From her childhood days in rural Finland, making tiny garments for dolls, through teen years sewing her own designs for friends, and on to adult life designing and sewing for pleasure and business, Leila Albala has combined her love of creative sewing with practical wearability. Upon graduation from Finnish commercial college, Leila worked in several European countries, gaining experience in a variety of jobs. When she and her husband, Elie, came to Canada in 1973, they founded their own mail order business, named ALPEL. Their self publishing business started in 1982. While sewing constantly for her children, Albert and Rina, Leila developed her own patterns and an easy way to design and print them in miniature. Her first book, "Easy Sewing for Infants", became an instant success after it was featured in Family Circle, Vogue Patterns, and dozens of other magazines. Thereafter, positive feedback from her readers inspired Leila to continue the series with "Easy Sewing for Children", "Easy Sewing for Adults", and "Easy Halloween Costumes for Children". Her next title will be "Easy Sewing for Teens".

Author photo by Elie Albala